MIRROR
MIRROR

Self-portraits by women artists

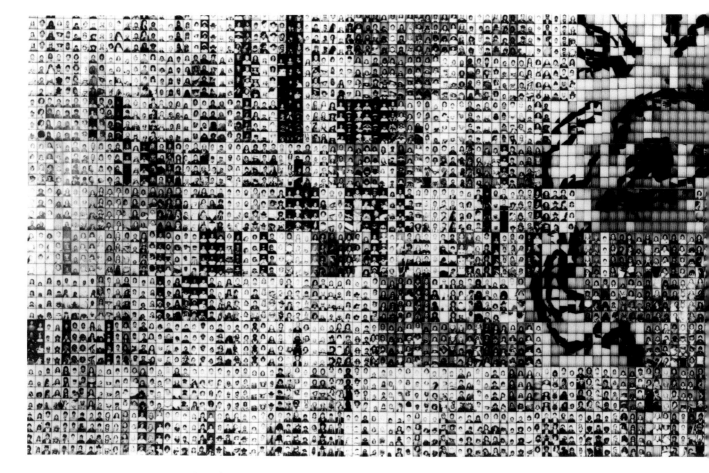

Liz Rideal (b.1954)
Identity, 1985
Laminated photo-booth strips on rag paper, 2000 x 5000mm (78¾ x 196⅞")
National Portrait Gallery, London (NPG D11008)

This mass self-portrait work, which includes a larger self-portrait of Liz Rideal within the main body of images, consists entirely of 1,220 photographic strips, making 4,880 individual portraits. During the summer of 1985, a photo-booth was installed at the National Portrait Gallery and members of the public were invited to 'disguise or reveal themselves'. The resulting performances were collaged together and featured on the *Wogan* television show on 27 September 1985. The work also includes self-portraits by Helen Chadwick and Maggi Hambling, and questions traditional self-portrait notions of authorship and collaboration.

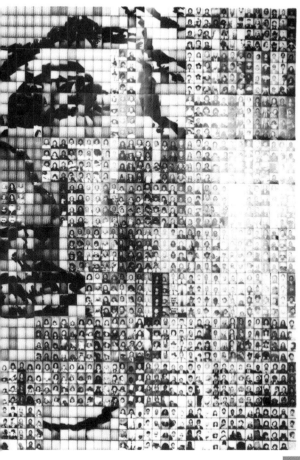

MIRROR
MIRROR

Self-portraits by women artists

Liz Rideal

with essays by Whitney Chadwick and Frances Borzello

WATSON-GUPTILL PUBLICATIONS / NEW YORK

First published in the United States in 2002 by Watson-Guptill Publications,
770 Broadway, New York, NY, 10003, www.watsonguptill.com

First published in Great Britain in 2001 by National Portrait Gallery Publications,
National Portrait Gallery, St Martin's Place, London WC2H 0HE

Published to accompany the exhibition *Mirror Mirror: Self-portraits by Women Artists* held at the
National Portrait Gallery, London, from 24 October 2001 to 24 February 2002.

ISBN 0-8230-3071-7

Library of Congress Control Number: 2001093863

Editor: Susie Foster
Production: Ruth Müller-Wirth
Design: Paul Vater at sugarfreedesign.co.uk
Printed by Butler & Tanner Limited, England

The publisher would like to thank the copyright holders for granting permission to reproduce works illustrated in this book.
Every effort has been made to contact the holders of copyright material, and any omissions will be corrected in future
editions if the publisher is notified in writing.

Front cover: Anna Zinkeisen, self-portrait, *c.*1944 (detail)
Back cover: Angelica Kauffmann, self-portrait, *c.*1770–5 (detail)

1 2 3 4 5 6 7 8 9 / 10 09 08 07 06 05 04 03 02

MIRROR
MIRROR
Contents

Acknowledgements

It is an honour to share this book with Frances Borzello and Whitney Chadwick and I have pleasure in thanking them for their eloquent texts.

At the National Portrait Gallery, I would like to thank my editor Susie Foster; the Exhibitions Manager, Beatrice Hosegood; Jacky Colliss Harvey; my researcher Rosemary Evison; Terence Pepper and Clare Freestone from the Gallery's Photographic Archive; the staff of the PR and Development Department, especially Pim Baxter, Bernadette O'Sullivan, Emma Marlow and Hazel Sutherland. I would like to thank Robin Gibson OBE, who made valuable comments on my text, and Paul Vater from *sugarfree* for his elegant book design. I would also like to thank those who have generously loaned works to the Gallery for the show and, most of all, the artists – without whom there would have been no exhibition.

When I first came to work at the National Portrait Gallery in 1982 I gravitated naturally towards the self-portraits on display. These images are the essence of our artistic heritage, reflecting the aspirations, styles and self-analytical states of artists who have been producing portraits in Britain since the sixteenth century. In isolating the self-portraits by women from the Gallery's collection, I wished to facilitate a study of this genre. I also invited contemporary women artists who had previous connections with the National Portrait Gallery to loan works for the show. The exhibition became the perfect opportunity to encourage new acquisitions for the Gallery, hence the addition of works by Helen Chadwick, Lee Miller and Doris Zinkeisen, as represented here, as well as other artists including Oriel Ross, Pamela Chandler, Tracey Emin and Sarah Lucas.

I am delighted that Leeds City Art Gallery agreed to lend their self-portrait by Milly Childers and that the Trustees of the Marie-Louise von Motesiczky Charitable Trust also agreed to loan her self-portrait. I would like to thank Richard Shone for suggesting the Vanessa Bell self-portrait that was kindly lent by a private London collector (it was sadly too late to include it in this book). These three paintings exemplify a period style; they are all vibrantly colourful personal works and have been an asset to the exhibition.

I am grateful to have had the opportunity to organise an exhibition that focuses mainly on the National Portrait Gallery's excellent permanent collection and, by drawing attention to it, encourage its expansion and celebrate its breadth.

Liz Rideal

Foreword

This is the first exhibition of women's self-portraits held at the National Portrait Gallery. It is a timely and thought-provoking investigation of a set of self-portraits, many of which have been drawn from the Gallery's own rich collections.

At least two of these portraits are amongst the greatest works in the collection – I would include the self-confident image that Gwen John painted of herself just after her return to London from Paris, and the striking, complex image of Laura Knight and her friend Ella Naper, which was painted in Newlyn just before the outbreak of World War I. Several of these self-portraits have been acquired by the Gallery recently, including those of Doris Zinkeisen, Jessica Dismorr and Helen Chadwick, the last of which was generously presented to the collection by Terence Pepper, our photography curator. It is excellent that we are able to show these works together as a group, in such a way as to suggest historical, social and artistic narratives. And it is particularly appropriate that the frontispiece to this book should be a photowork by Liz Rideal, who organised the exhibition for us.

Charles Saumarez Smith
Director

How Do I Look?
Whitney Chadwick

> I now began to feel that having finished with Art School I must leave the student stage and become an artist … I painted a still-life portrait of myself in the looking glass. The colour was very dull but it was very well drawn.
> (Nina Hamnett, *Laughing Torso*, 1932)

Nina Hamnett (1890–1956) 'became an artist' in 1911, accepting a commission from the poet and magician Aleister Crowley (1875–1947) and exhibiting for the first time with the Allied Artists Association at the Royal Albert Hall. Despite these early signs of professional success, the transition from the familiar world of the 'lady art student' to the less well-charted territory of the professional woman artist cannot have been easy. Like Narcissus before her, Hamnett turned to the reflected image for access to an 'other', a self defined in and through representation.

It is not surprising to enter a picture gallery and find it filled with images of women, a few of which may even have been executed by a woman's hand. But it is noteworthy, even today, to confront an entire exhibition of women's self-portraits. Contemplating the works in *Mirror Mirror*, I am struck by the steady gazes on display, by the refusal of these artists who are also women to cede the act of viewing entirely to the voyeuristic gazes of others. If there is little radical stylistic experimentation here, there is also little evidence of that combination of surface richness and interior vacuousness we have come to associate with femininity displayed on museum walls. Instead the women in these representations confront us directly: whimsical, earnest, studious, enigmatic, flamboyant, shy, visionary. Beauty and identity, two of art history's most difficult and unstable categories, are summoned forth across a dazzling range of costumes, gestures, looks, poses, materials and presentations.

It is, above all, an historical collection and one must wonder what it tells us – about women painting themselves, about women artists and history, about Englishness. It suggests many, and often contradictory, things reinforcing a history of European art in which artists were most often white and middle class, but overturning gender assumptions that might lead us to believe that they were also almost always men. Biographical sketches provide histories of families and immigration patterns, and records of institutional access and training, but the images themselves are often difficult to interpret. Thinking about how to construct a narrative around such a diversity of styles and historical periods, where to generalise and how to avoid over-determined meaning and reductive conclusions, I am reminded of art historian Linda Nochlin's early caution against assuming that gender alone is sufficient reason to assume stylistic (or conceptual, or political, or ideological) affinity. 'In every instance,' she warned in her pioneering feminist essay of 1971, 'Why Have There Been No Great Women Artists?', 'women artists and writers would seem to be closer to other artists and writers of their own period and outlook than they are to each other.'[1]

Subsequent feminist scholarship has confirmed the limitations of a belief in the unifying power of female nature or a feminine essence, and alerted us to the complex workings of sexual difference in representation. Nevertheless, a gallery full of self-portraits by women artists demands thinking about in terms of points of connection as well as divergence. Despite differences in historical context, medium, artistic style and intention – not to mention the mediating factors of class, ethnicity, age and sexual orientation – there are surely commonalities here: links between gender and representational strategies, reworkings of the historical incompatibility between the role of woman and that of artist, shared struggles among women to define themselves as professionals in a world that has historically offered them few role models and even less space for explorations of otherness. I am interested in what these self-portraits might tell us about the relationship between the fixed image and female subjectivity, or the ways that femininity is internalised as an effect of the same surfaces and artifices that construct our notions of the beautiful, or how women artists have negotiated the territory that lies between the categories of 'images of women' and 'images of the woman artist'. I want to return to these issues not to resolve them, for in every case they resist easy answers, but rather to explore how they have contributed to shaping the awareness of self that lies at the heart of any exhibition of self-portraits.

Every woman who paints a self-portrait, or sculpts a likeness, or places herself in front of the lens of a camera whose shutter she controls, challenges in some way the complex relationship that exists between masculine agency and feminine passivity in Western art history. I like to think that in taking up brush or pen, chisel or camera, women assert a claim to the representation of women (as opposed to Woman) that Western culture long ago ceded to male genius and patriarchal perspectives, and that in turning to the image in the mirror they take another step towards the elaboration of a sexualised subjective female identity. Indeed I prefer that view to the nagging fear that many women's self-portraits arose out of, as Nina Hamnett suggests, simply not knowing where to go next.

In *The Second Sex* (1946), Simone de Beauvoir (1908–86) structured sexual difference and self-identification around the reflected image. 'Man,' she suggests, 'feeling and wishing himself active, subject, does not see himself in his fixed image; it has little attraction for him, since man's body does not seem to him an object of desire; while woman, knowing and making herself object, believes she really sees *herself* in the glass.' De Beauvoir's words resonate uneasily in an era in which mass media and popular culture play a growing role in constructing and mediating our relationship to the world and to the categories through which we define ourselves (including gender, race, age, class, beauty and occupation), and psychoanalysts and academic feminists continue to challenge both the notions of fixed identity and the psychic integration she implies. Yet a belief in the visuality of feminine self-identification, and the power of the image to mediate between art object and human subject, continues to endow the self-portrait with its power to work on our imaginations.[2]

That Nina Hamnett should link the question of becoming an artist to an interrogation of her own reflected image suggests a lack of existing representations uniting the categories of woman and artist. For young women artists in 1911 – or, say, in 1780 or 1870 – there were precious few examples about, despite the fact that debates about the public role and image of the male artist had preoccupied critics and historians, not to mention artists, at least since the Renaissance. Hamnett was one of a generation of young English women born between 1890 and 1906 whose professional ambitions were nurtured in a world of changing social conditions for middle-class women that began with the Divorce Act of 1857 and the Married Women's Property Act of 1870, and culminated in the suffrage campaigns of the Edwardian era. Increased opportunities for middle-class women included education reforms that led to the admission of women to the Royal Academy of Arts, the Slade School of Fine Art (founded 1871) and the Government Schools of Design.

Among other women of this generation included in this book are the painters Eileen Agar (1899–1991), Paule Vézelay (1892–1984), Gluck (1895–1978), Marie-Louise von Motesiczky (1906–96) and Anna and Doris Zinkeisen (1901–76 and 1898–1991), the sculptor Dame Barbara Hepworth (1903–75) and the printmaker, sculptor and illustrator Gertrude Hermes (1901–83). Their self-portraits attest to expanded opportunities for women, as well as to the high degree of technical training they received in their courses of study. The changing social landscape helps to explain why the National Portrait Gallery's collection of self-portraits by women artists opens out so dramatically in numbers as we move into the late nineteenth and twentieth centuries. It explains the expanded roles available to many women, but it doesn't answer Hamnett's question.

The first formulation of the new ideal of the artist as a learned man, and the work of art as the unique expression of a gifted individual, appeared in Leon Battista Alberti's treatise *On Painting*, first published in 1435. As the identification of the male artist as a

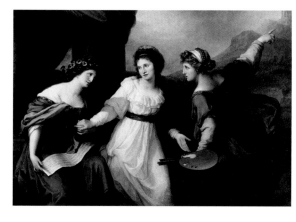

1.
The Artist Hesitating Between the Arts of Music and Painting
Angelica Kauffmann
(1741–1807), indistinctly dated
1794
Oil on canvas,
1475 x 2185mm (58 x 86")
Nostell Priory (The National Trust)

learned gentleman grew more secure, women artists from Sofonisba Anguissola (*c.*1532–1625) to Lavinia Fontana (1552–1614) were also expected to display the signs of respectable femininity in their self-images. Yet the categories of woman and artist, as the art historian Griselda Pollock and others have shown, remained incompatible, and many of the self-portraits in this book reveal an ongoing struggle to reconcile cultural constructions of femininity with what it has meant to be an artist and a woman at specific historical moments.

Mary Beale's imposing self-portrait of *c.*1665 (see p.35) was painted during a period of transition between puritanical prohibitions against 'frivolities', including the public performance of plays, and greater social freedom. John Evelyn's (1620–1706) comment of 1654 that 'the Women beegan to paint themselves, formerly a most ignominious thing, and used onely by prostitutes'[3] refers to the application of make-up, but there exists a strong rhetorical link between using paint to 'make-up' femininity in reality and in representation. Beale's painting draws from a wide range of sources in producing its image of the first Englishwoman to become a portrait painter of distinction. In composition and pose, as well as in its muted tonalities, the portrait owes much to Sir Anthony van Dyck (1599–1641) and Sir Peter Lely (1618–80). Its imagery of feminine physicality and self-possession recalls Italian baroque images of the female heroine, and the colouristic richness of its flowing draperies points towards the next century's glittering achievements in

English portrait painting. If there is pride in Beale's contemplation of a mirror that reflects back the image of a dignified and successful woman artist, there is also a suggestion that the image she has chosen to present here has been carefully constructed. The palette that hangs on the wall and the unframed canvas on which her strong right hand rests speak of her professional stature. The image of her two sons in the unfinished painting indicates confidence in her ability to unite the roles of artist, wife and mother (it can't have hurt that by 1669 Charles Beale was running the household and looked after the family's business affairs while his wife painted).

A century later, Swiss-born Angelica Kauffmann set about clothing her ambition to be accepted as an history painter, the highest level of academic achievement, in the desirable feminine traits of modesty, charm and accomplishment. 'Look at me,' the finger that points to her breast in the self-portrait of *c*.1770–5 (see p.37) seems to say, 'for I am capable of charm and more.' Indeed nowhere is the difficulty of differentiating between the image of the woman artist and that of the beautiful woman more clearly articulated than in a genre of eighteenth-century self-portraits in which women artists advertised their skills through flattering depictions of self. Kauffmann's late self-portrait *The Artist Hesitating Between the Arts of Music and Painting* (fig.1) takes its theme from the classical story of Hercules' choice between Pleasure and Virtue, and shows the artist as a young woman hesitating between gentle Music and powerful Painting. According to her biographer Frances A. Gerard, Kauffmann was equally talented as a musician and a painter. Her later characterisation of herself, drawn from the traditions both of biography and portrait painting, enabled her to fuse the virtues of ambition and hard work with images of femininity, but at a price – the visual distinction between the individual woman and the allegorical female figures collapses.

No such problem confronted Kauffmann's male contemporaries, as self-portraits by Sir Joshua Reynolds in England and Jean-Baptiste-Siméon Chardin in France suggest. Reynolds' *Portrait of the Artist* (fig.2) reveals neither hesitation nor self-doubt in its characterisation of the President of the Royal Academy as an academic man. He displays himself in the robes of his honorary doctorate from the University of Oxford, an academic award he received not because of his status as a painter, but because of the brilliance of the scholarly discourses on art that he regularly delivered to his fellow academicians. His place within a lineage of masculine genius that can be traced to the Renaissance reclassification of the artist from craftsman to educated gentleman is secured by the inclusion of a bust of his hero, Michelangelo (1475–1564). By contrast Chardin, in his pastel *Self-portrait* or *Portrait of Chardin Wearing an Eyeshade* (1775; fig.3), appears to eschew the external signs of genius. Nevertheless, he has no difficulty in convincing the viewer of his place within an historical trajectory as he transforms the infirmities of old age into a radical and individuated meditation on hard work and age.

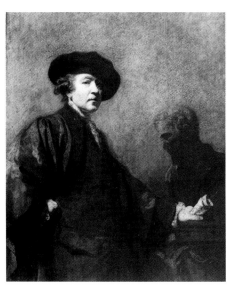

2.
Portrait of the Artist
Sir Joshua Reynolds
(1723–92), 1780
Oil on panel,
1270 x 1016mm (50 x 40")
Royal Academy of Arts, London

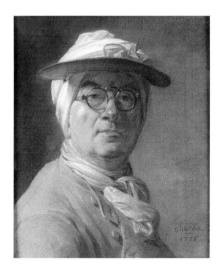

3.
Self-portrait
Jean-Baptiste-Siméon
Chardin (1699–1779), 1775
Pastel, 460 x 380mm
(18 x 15")
Cabinet des Dessins,
Louvre, Paris

The subject of the artist as old woman does not feature prominently among the National Portrait Gallery's collection of female self-portraits, for women in Western culture have had little to gain from embracing images of the ageing body. Among the self-portraits painted between the 1860s and the 1930s, the majority depict women in their late twenties and thirties, self-possessed and earnest, and looking forward with an air of expectation rather than back at lives already lived. For the most part, they avoid making strong psychological demands on the viewer in favour of offering likeable images for our contemplation. These range from Ann Mary Newton's modest presentation of herself holding a portfolio, a painting that moved the *Spectator* critic to note that there was 'no better lady's portrait than Mrs Newton's portrait of herself' in the Royal Academy exhibition of 1863, to Elizabeth, Lady Butler's, sober painting of 1869 and Gwen John's self-portrait of *c.*1900, with its air of watchful superiority (see pp.41, 43, 49). John's portrait, like so many others in this book, was painted at the beginning of her artistic career and serves more to announce the seriousness of her intentions than to reveal the workings of her inner life.

Self-portraits executed during the first decades of the twentieth century continue the tradition of careful scrutiny and long meditation that led Sir Ernst Gombrich (b.1909) to observe that 'the correct portrait … is an end product on a long road through schema and correction. It is not a faithful record of a visual experience but a faithful construction of a relational model.'[4] Several of them, including Eileen Agar's loosely painted post-Impressionist self-portrait of 1927 and Paule Vézelay's muted and quasi-abstract self-image of *c.*1927–9 (see pp.63 and 65), link the conventions of the self-portrait to the artists' adherence to modernist styles from post-Impressionism to Cubism.

Self-portraits by women artists draw us into the problematics of deciphering the identity that lies behind the social expectation that women present themselves in public adorned, masked and made-up. Not only does the act of painting a self-portrait (unlike the taking of a photograph) engage us with a practice that requires the translation of sensations, but the fact of basing the representation on a reflected image imposes its own conditions. Structuring representational and interpretative possibilities, the mirror, functioning as a screen for projecting onto, maintains a distance without the possibility of mediation. 'The mirror,' writes psychoanalyst Luce Irigaray

> … almost always serves to reduce us to a pure exteriority − of a very particular kind. It functions as a possible way to constitute screens between the other and myself. In a way quite different from mucuses or skin, living, porous, fluid differentiations and the possibility of communion, the mirror is a weapon of frozen − and polemical − distancing.[5]

This tension between identification and otherness contributes to the difficulty of interpreting the self-portrait. As viewers we are both seduced into assuming a kind of 'intimacy' with the sitter, and distanced by the fixity of a representation so at odds with the fluidity of our normal social relationships. A number of the artists in this book have chosen to emphasise the signs of social life in their representations, or to engage directly with the difficulty of reconciling images of femininity as something-to-be-looked-at with representations of the artist, historically produced around attributes signifying masculinity: ambition, daring, individualism. Anna Zinkeisen's self-portrait of *c.*1944 (see p.85) balances the head with its carefully made-up face, plucked eyebrows and stylish coiffure against an image of painting as a physically demanding practice, asserted here through her rolled-up sleeves, the powerful arm and hand that grasps the brushes, and the monumentality implied by the lowered viewpoint. Stylistically, the painting links the signs of class, visible in the figure's self-confident individualism, with those of the artist's scientific interest in pathological and clinical drawing and her war work as a nurse. Olive Edis's photographic self-portrait of 1918 (see p.59) also mixes signs of the professional and the personal. She displays her National War Museum badge above multiple strands of pearls, and photographs herself holding a camera and wearing the uniform she designed when she was commissioned to record the work of the British Women's Services in France and Flanders during World War I.

Edis's photographic portrait points up the difference that medium makes. Its apparent spontaneity and suggestion of a captured moment, and the quick jolt of recognition that accompanies our acceptance of the photographic image as closer to the real (and by extension to our own) world than the painting, shape our reading. Moreover the photographer's casual air, and reliance on a pose that would be difficult to hold long enough for the production of a painting, calls attention to the attenuated process that Gombrich identifies with the painted self-portrait with its mirror-image reversal of left and right, its abstraction, its fixity in time and space.

Perhaps the most radical engagement with the conventions of painting from life can be seen in Dame Laura Knight's (1877–1970) self-portrait of 1913 (p.57). The artist has chosen to show herself from the back, brush in hand, contemplating a posed naked female model whose position in relation to both artist and spectator suggests her removal to the kind of space of display most often associated with the spectacle of the windows of large department stores:

> The first time I saw it, I completely misread the image. Failing to notice the brush in the artist's right hand, I thought I was seeing a woman looking through the window of a gallery or shop. This mistake seems to me to be revealing of certain cultural assumptions about femininity. While the woman's narcissistic glance in a mirror or a shop window is socially legitimated, her critical and investigative gaze is not.[6]

Art historian Rosemary Betterton goes on to suggest that while the picture does not produce the voyeurism usual in representations of the female nude, neither does it offer the viewer any other coherent viewing position, at least in part because the relationship between woman artist and woman model transgresses the normative roles of male and female, artist and model, clothed and naked, the one who looks and the one who is looked at.[7] The painter's incorporation of the relationship between artist and model and the visual dynamics of working from life in the studio into her self-representation contrasts sharply with many other depictions of studio practice.

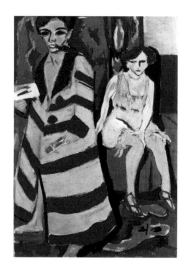

4.
Self-portrait with Model
Ernst Ludwig Kirchner
(1880–1938), *c.*1910,
overpainted 1926
Oil on canvas,
1504 x 1000mm
(59¼ x 39⅜")
Hamburger Kunsthalle

In Ernst Ludwig Kirchner's Expressionist *Self-portrait with Model* (fig.4) the image of the painter, wrapped in a voluminous and garishly striped bathrobe and observed by a scantily clad model who sits behind him on a bed, dominates the canvas. The inequality of the power relations that exist between the male artist and his female model is articulated through his physical domination of the pictorial space, the sexuality implicit in his apparent nudity and the brush that points suggestively in the direction of his genitals, the overheated palette and powerful application of paint. The fact that Knight's model was an artist friend and neighbour, the wife of painter Charles Naper, erases both the model's anonymity and the class differences between artists and their models that have structured painting practices in Western art. Knight's painting, like Kirchner's, resonates with reds and oranges, but here they serve to warm Ella Naper's flesh and intensify an overall mood of intimacy rather than one of sexual conquest.

Knight's situating of the artist's self-representation within a studio environment understood as a space of social relations as well as individual actions alludes to the social dimensions of self-representation. A sense of the theatrical, an awareness of the staging of the self for the painting, often accompanies portrait painting generally, and the self-portrait in particular, for the latter above all other forms of painting engages with issues of self-definition and self-identity. Often these are elicited through an emphasis on the constructed nature of artistic practice with its reliance on materials, props, furniture and work spaces.

The world's a theatre, the earth a stage
Which God and Nature do with actors fill
(**Thomas Heywood**, *Apology for Actors*, 1612)

The self-portrait turns on the staging of the self (the model) for the self (the artist). For the woman artist, the difficulty and paradox of being both active, creative subject – a maker of meaning – and passive object – a site of meaning – can only be resolved through performing the self. While the image itself remains fixed, a complex of looks – those of the artist, the camera, the image, the spectator – produces multiple subject positions, and distinctions between seer and seen, subject of the gaze and object of it, artist and model, begin to break down.[8]

Photographic *mise-en-scène*, the staging of a scene for the camera, encourages the production of intricate fictions, diverse selves, dramas of fantasy and desire. Painting also encourages self-construction through a reiteration of legible signs, and the use of camera or mirror may encourage the manipulation of these signs. Many nineteenth-century photographs display this new medium's reliance on the visual and compositional conventions of both painting and theatre. A photograph published in 1899 and thought to be a self-portrait by Lallie Charles in her studio with her two sisters (see p.47) offers a view into a late Victorian sitting-room that resembles an elaborate stage set, an effect encouraged by the carefully posed family group with their intersecting gazes. The scene's narrative implications rest on the implicit interaction between individual figures and between figures and viewer and the careful arrangement of screens, pillows, teacups and small objets d'art.

In our own century, one of endlessly proliferating photographic images, it is not the world that is the stage, but the space carved out between the body, the camera and our acceptance of the mediated image as providing our primary access to the world. Dorothy Wilding's (1893–1976) purchase of her first view camera and tripod in 1909, when she was sixteen years old, seems to have been prompted by the current vogue for collecting picture postcards of actors and actresses of the day. To the stage-struck adolescent, these pictures provided the catalyst for her first experiments with blanket backdrops, carefully arranged in the family garden, and the use of oak chests to imitate the 'old master' ambience then fashionable in studio photography. Her 1930s self-portrait (see p.73), in which she appears ready to leap from behind her cumbersome apparatus, collapses the visual conventions of theatre, dance and pin-up postcard without revealing anything much about the artist beyond the appearance of animation and *joie de vivre*.

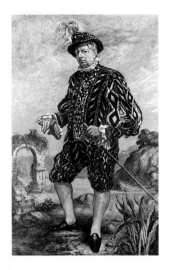

5.
Self-portrait in Black Costume
Giorgio de Chirico
(1888–1978), 1948
Oil on canvas,
1525 x 980mm (60 x 38⅝")
Galleria Nazionale d'Arte
Moderna di Roma

Italian painter Giorgio de Chirico's late series of parodies on historical self-portrait traditions derive much of their effect from a contemporary familiarity with visual traditions of burlesque and caricature. In *Self-portrait in the Costume of an Eighteenth-century Gentleman* (1954) and *Self-portrait in Black Costume* (fig.5), de Chirico takes on the visual representation of the artist as gentleman and exposes the self-consciousness of many earlier representations in this mode, including Reynolds' 1780 *Portrait of the Artist*, to which the former bears a close relationship (see p.11). The essential theatricality of such self-staging finds echoes in the elaborate visual productions of many contemporary artists, here including (though expressed in very different ways) those of Maggi Hambling (b.1945), Jo Spence (1934–92) and Helen Chadwick (1953–96), each of which exposes the fictive nature of its medium, whether painting, photography or xerographic reproduction.

Maggi Hambling's self-portrait of 1977–8 (see p.97) is as much about the explicit representation of the artist's distinctive style as it is about capturing a 'likeness'. Its effect depends not on accuracy of drawing (the figure exhibits three arms, each of them engaged in a different activity) to reveal the self, but on a kind of schematic symbolic narrative, an accumulation of meaningful images and details that situate the self within a specific environment: 'My love life was in a muddle when I painted this, over twenty years ago,' the artist remarked recently:

> I was confused and the muddle confronts the viewer … What I like is that it's quite raw. The muddle was occupying me, but there's probably something in all these animals, birds and objects which reminded me that life goes on. The world is large and one is very small.[9]

In Hambling's painting, detailed rendering jostles with near abstraction, and abrupt dislocations of scale and spatial relations combine with lush areas of paint application and flat, uninflected expanses of background. The result is a disquieting image of the artist at work in a studio that appears less as a discrete and comprehensible architectural space than as a screen across which flows a string of almost cinematic images. Hambling's painting calls attention to the interwoven relationship between visible world, biography, memory, fantasy and psychology that defines her artistic practice. The artist appears at the centre of this complex of images, jostling for space with the cat that has laid claim to her chair, the bird that streaks across her face, and in a juggling act that enables her to smoke, paint and drink while contemplating a nude model and giving free rein to the mental images that surround her.

Helen Chadwick's self-portrait of 1986 (see p.101) was made as a companion piece to her installation at the Institute of Contemporary Arts, *Of Mutability*. This installation, a composite image produced from a mosaic of hundreds of individual photocopies, also calls attention to the constructed nature of representation and artistic self-identity. 'The title really is the cue for a concept of the self as being infinitely subject to change,' the artist explained in a 1989 interview. 'There is a continuity but in perpetual shifting, of the notions of what we are through what we feel. There are emblems of decay in *Of Mutability* but equally there are emblems of renewal.'

Of Mutability's large scale (reinforced by the fact that the spectator views the piece from a raised platform) recalls its sources in the painted decorations of baroque and rococo buildings, many of which contain their own panoramas of symbolic and mythological images. Yet for all its associations with age-old tropes of decay, regeneration, nature and culture, the piece is altogether contemporary in the ways it calls attention to the socially constructed nature of identity in a world of which our perception is endlessly mediated by reproductive technologies and multiple images.

It is Jo Spence's photographic self-portrait of 1990 (see p.103) that perhaps most boldly confronts one of the most hidden and taboo subjects in Western culture: death itself. Collapsing mythic generalisation and intimate self-revelation in a carefully staged but haunting image, Spence produced a deeply ironic meditation on the place of the female nude in Western representation. Her long battle with breast cancer is well-documented in both her photographs and her writing. In this series, she began to reuse older images and earlier work in manipulated images that compel a wide range of readings. The body Spence presents to the viewer is a body that demands that we read its signs of age, illness and disability against a series of historical representations: the mythic image of the Amazon, the single-breasted woman warrior; the idealised female nude of Western representation; the ancient crone. It is as if all of these representations of femininity have been locked together in an endless dance of life and death. 'I realised with horror that my body was not made of photographic paper,' Spence wrote in her autobiography *Putting Myself in the Picture* (1986), '… nor was it an image or an idea, or a psychic structure … it was made of blood, bones, and tissue.'

Spence's photograph belongs to a body of work that emerged out of a radical feminist photographic initiative she developed during the 1980s with her collaborator Rosy Martin, in which repressed feelings, past experiences and memories were made visible through a process of restaging them in front of the camera. Recreating their own histories as tableaux, Spence and Martin (and others with whom Spence collaborated on various photographic series) used the camera as a tool through which to examine the realities of class, sexuality, work, family and illness.

Under this mask, another mask. I will never be finished carrying all these faces.
(**Claude Cahun**, *Aveus non Avenus*, 1930)

Masking and masquerade, like *mise-en-scène*, encourage the production of intricate fictions. They have been deployed to challenge the boundaries of gender and sexual identities, as well as the temptation to accept the image as a transparent representation of a fixed reality. Both are linked to the concept of the carnivalesque 'body' of medieval and Renaissance popular culture as described in the work of the twentieth-century Russian literary theorist Mikhail Bakhtin. In Belgian painter James Ensor's *Self-portrait with Masks* (fig.6) the painter's face – his individuality – both stands out from and is slowly consumed by a proliferation of masks that press in on it until we are no longer certain where the man ends and the mask begins. Ensor's masked figures are associated with Lenten carnivals, a time when masking enables the release of powerful feelings that must otherwise be contained within fixed social behaviours.

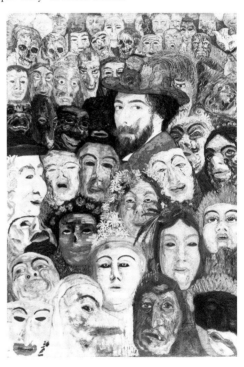

6.
Self-portrait with Masks
James Ensor
(1860–1949), 1899
Oil on canvas,
1170 x 800mm (46⅛ x 31½")
Menard Art Museum,
Aichi, Japan

By temporarily dislodging identities normally fixed by social rules, masking and masquerade have provided women artists with new ways of bringing femininity into representation. Many women artists in the twentieth century have employed cross-dressing and androgyny as strategies through which to challenge and/or unfix the categories of gender and sexuality and introduce ambiguity and fluidity.[10] Androgyny became an important means of reassessing the dynamics of lesbian identity in early twentieth-century visual and literary culture. Medical models that viewed homosexuality as a 'third sex' combining elements of masculinity and femininity shaped the use of androgynous images by painters from Romaine Brooks (1874–1970) to Gluck, and by writers such as Radclyffe Hall (1880–1943), Natalie Barney (1876–1972), and others. The English painter Hannah Gluckstein, known as Gluck (or Peter), an acquaintance of Brooks and Barney, is the subject of Brooks' painting of 1923–4 entitled *Peter, a Young English Girl*. The painting shows her in profile with close cropped hair and finely chiselled features, her slender cross-dressed form enveloped in a large black overcoat.

Gluck's own paintings point to similar concerns with theatricality and androgyny. The series of paintings called *Stage and Country*, included in her first major solo exhibition in 1926 at the Fine Art Society in London, depicted specific London stage entertainers. They point to her interest in the construction of self through manipulations of the external signs of class, occupation and sexuality. Art historian Joe Lucchesi, who has written widely on the Brooks, Barney, Gluck circle, notes that these 'stage' paintings underscore 'the blurred lines between theatrical performance and the performative artifice of London's theatre society … In these paintings everything and everyone remains behind masks, costumes, screens and

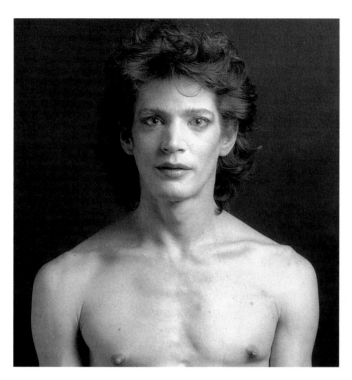

7.
Self-portrait
Robert Mapplethorpe
(1946–89), 1980
Gelatin silver print,
508 x 406mm (20 x 16")
The Estate of Robert
Mapplethorpe

props under the harsh glare of public scrutiny.'[11] Gluck's self-portrait of 1942 (see p.81) suggests the artist's ongoing interest in the ability of the self-portrait to both reveal and conceal. The head, with its closely cropped hair, strong jaw and direct gaze, appears rigid and locked to the picture plane, giving the figure the expression of isolated individualism that also informs many of Romaine Brooks' portraits. Signs of class and social privilege can be observed in the artist's choice of a meticulously naturalistic style of representation, her expression of defiant control, and the decision to assume the slightly elevated viewpoint and expression of haughty superiority often associated with representations of male British landed gentry.[12]

Gluck's image both projects and conceals the figure's sexuality – reserved, potentially transgressive, held under rigid control and subject to the operations of class privilege. It anticipates late twentieth-century popular culture's reliance on manipulating the signs through which we read sexual identity in constructing the images of transgendering and transexuality that form a large segment of fashionable pop culture, from David Bowie to Michael Jackson. Robert Mapplethorpe's photographic self-portrait (fig.7) relies on a similar fusing of the signs of masculinity and femininity. Here the artist exposes an upper torso with a well-defined musculature that recalls the ideal male nudes of classical Greek sculpture, while at the same time withdrawing behind the provocative and androgynous beauty of a carefully controlled, mask-like face which signals its feminised desire through large eyes, luxuriantly curled long hair and slightly parted lips.

Masquerade also plays an important role in psychoanalytic literature. Joan Rivière's classic essay 'Womanliness as Masquerade', first published in 1929, describes a defensive posture in which women may adopt a mask of excessive femininity as a defence when entering professional spaces defined by male power and privilege. Caught in a trap in which a masquerading womanliness is also defined as 'the essence of femininity', of what it is to be a woman, she manages only to signify that she is 'not-a-woman'. For Rivière, writing in the early years of the popularising of Freud's theories of sexuality in Europe and North America, the motivations for the masquerade of femininity were unconscious defences against sexual anxiety. More recently, feminist film critics have theorised the role of masquerade in women's flaunting of femininity as a means of undermining patriarchal viewing positions and norms.

If Rivière's masquerade of femininity enabled the woman to navigate a social territory of male fetishisms and female sexuality, Lucy Schwob, who created the alter ego of 'Claude Cahun', manipulated photographic images of herself as Cahun, costumed, disguised and/or masked (fig.8), which comprise one of the century's first coherent bodies of work by a woman artist to call into question the very possibility of a unified self. Cahun moved in vanguard circles in Paris during the 1920s and 1930s, and her iconography of a fluid transgendered identity derived both from that city's pioneering lesbian culture and avant-garde theatre in the 1920s, and from the Dada and Surrealist explorations of sexuality and androgyny evident in Marcel Duchamp's (1887–1968) gender-bending reinvention of himself through his alter ego Rose Sélavy. Articulating gender and sexuality as positional rather than fixed, Cahun's self-representations continually return us to the ways that images, even those based on the most personal aspects of our self-identity, derive their meaning in the world from the complex sets of social and cultural signs and codes on which we depend to make that world legible.

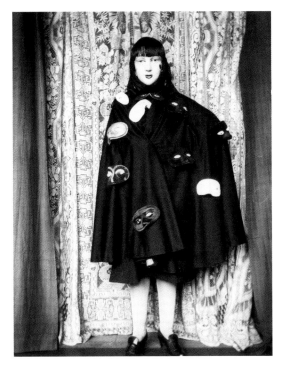

8.
Self-portrait (in robes with masks attached)
Claude Cahun
(1894–1954), *c.*1928
Modern print from an original negative,
177 x 127mm (7 x 5")
Jersey Museum

It is also possible to exaggerate the signs of femininity until it becomes almost impossible to locate a 'self' in the artifice of display and surface elaboration. Nowhere is the line between woman and object more skilfully articulated than in Susie Cooper's self-portrait ceramic mask of *c.*1933 (see p.75). Here the designer's skill as a ceramicist and painter is turned to the fashioning of an image of the self as an object. Yet the impression of the woman as a beautiful object, a construction that underlies a historical tradition of porcelain manufacture, begins to dissolve on closer inspection. Cooper's image, though exaggeratedly stylised, is not idealised. It calls attention to the face's asymmetry, the misalignment of eyes set deeply into the head, the uneven application of red lipstick. The perfect object quickly collapses into the deformed object.

A projection of the woman as decorative surface and object can also be seen in painter and stage-designer Doris Zinkeisen's self-portrait, exhibited in 1929 (see p.67). Working in a manner that became closely associated with the stylisations of modern fashion and theatre design in the 1920s, Zinkeisen's theatrical flair is evident in her self-presentation as a perfectly marcelled mannequin, an elegant armature on which to display the brilliantly patterned silk shawl. Posed against a simple ivory drape, the icy tones of the flesh relieved only by the application of rouge, lipstick and eyeshadow become a foil for the dramatic gown with its explosion of intensely coloured birds and tropical flowers. The other side of this kind of representation of self as surface and object is self-portrait traditions that engage with the subject's interior life and give form to the psychological or the visionary.

My Life is uneventful but I sometimes have an interesting Dream.
(**Ithell Colquhoun**, 1939)

Ithell Colquhoun (1906–88) relies on Surrealist techniques of automatism such as staining (applying a thin wash or ground that is absorbed into the canvas or paper and provides a mottled abstract field conducive to poetic association) to produce an image of self rich in suggestibility. Although the size of the eyes in her self-portrait thought to have been made in the 1930s (see p.71) is exaggerated, the gaze is not directed outwards. Rather it is turned inwards, towards 'that purely internal model' which the poet André Breton (1896–1966) posited in 1928 as the only legitimate source for the work of art.[13] Brooding and introverted, Colquhoun's image recalls her interest in reaching new levels of creative imagination through explorations of the dream and the unconscious, as well as by exploiting the rich imagery of alchemy and the magic arts.

Colquhoun's hermetic image, one of two studies in the collection of the National Portrait Gallery, stands in sharp contrast to society photographer Madame Yevonde's (1893–1975) projection of the photographic self-portrait as the result of a carefully staged process of visionary experimentation. Yevonde's self-portrait of 1940 (see p.79) captures her stylishly dressed figure within an elaborate gold frame, surrounded by objects that suggest both the science and the magic of photography and recall seventeenth-century *vanitas* painting. Her photograph of Dorothy, Duchess of Wellington, as Hecate from her 1935 series 'Goddesses' rests on top of the frame. The presence of Hecate, the Greek goddess who haunted graveyards, reinforces the work's content as a meditation on the transitoriness of life (suggested by the butterflies) and the magical allure of science (imaged here in the bottles of chemicals, the wires and other photographic apparatus). In the centre the photographer holds a negative up to the light as if magically conjuring an image.

It is perhaps unfair to juxtapose attempts to endow an image with hidden significance, such as those of Colquhoun and Yevonde, with the political commitment and social activism that shaped Sylvia Pankhurst's (1882–1960) artistic practice. Nevertheless all three self-images, each in its very different way, speak of challenges inherent in attempts to link self-identity to complex systems of meaning and social action in a single image. Pankhurst's life was increasingly characterised by the irreconcilability of her public struggles and private goals. As the Pankhursts' campaign for women's suffrage intensified after 1906, her artistic contributions to the movement, which included the prison sketches she published in the *Pall Mall Gazette* in 1907 after a period of incarceration, were often overshadowed by a growing conflict with her mother and sister over questions of strategy and focus. Torn between her political commitments and her life as an artist, she was increasingly unable to resolve this conflict. 'Art and politics pulled stubbornly apart for her,' Lisa Tickner writes in her comprehensive study of the imagery of the suffrage campaign, 'the project of working as an artist in the cause of the suffrage and of socialism was hard to realise.'[14] Within a couple of years, Tickner reports, Pankhurst had come to a decision and given up painting. Her pastel self-portrait (*c*.1906; see p.55) shows her dressed in what appears to be a prison uniform of loose smock and bonnet gazing upwards, mouth open, with an expression of visionary intensity. Her use of white chalk to heighten the work's psychological expressiveness recalls Samuel Palmer's *Self-portrait* (fig.9), in which the young man's brooding gaze is given a visionary unreality through the play of white highlights across the face. Pankhurst's image of all-consuming political commitment suggests her willingness to merge her self-identity with a larger cause. Pankhurst's drawing is almost alone among the National Portrait Gallery's female self-portraits (though she shares her commitment to political consciousness with Jo Spence) in defining herself through political and social activism.

Women are defined by history as well as biology, culture as well as nature. The self-portrait has offered women artists an opportunity to explore a complex and unstable visual territory in which their subjectivity and lived experience as women intersects with the visual language which has historically constructed 'woman' as object and other. Within this space, women have struggled to locate positions from which to speak and have renegotiated the relationship between subject and object. No single model of self-portraiture can stand for the experiences of women generally, or fully express the rich interplay that exists between the examination of the reflected image and the exploration of the social dimensions of lived experience, but self-representation remains critical to self-understanding and it plays a particularly important role in women's creative lives.

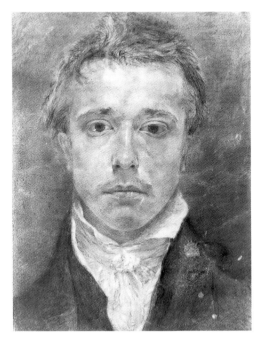

9.
Self-portrait
Samuel Palmer
(1805–81), *c.*1826
Black chalk heightened with white on buff paper,
291 x 229mm (11½ x 9")
Ashmolean Museum, Oxford

Notes

1. Nochlin, 1988, pp.145–78; the quote is on p.149.
2. Mieke Bal, 'Reading Art', in Pollock, 1996, p.25.
3. Cited in Piper, 1992, p.96.
4. Gombrich, 1977, pp.122–3.
5. Cited in Hilary Robinson, 'Whose Beauty? Women, Art, and Intersubjectivity in Luce Irigaray's Writings', in Brand, 2000, p.231.
6. Betterton, 1987, p.4.
7. Ibid., p.5.
8. For a discussion of the implications of these dynamics for photographic practice, see Solomon-Godeau, 1991, p.241 and *passim*.
9. 'The Sitter's Tale', *Independent on Sunday*, 8 January 1999.
10. Meskimmon, 1996, pp.102–50.
11. Joe Lucchesi, 'Gluck', in Gaze, 1997, pp. 585–7.
12. Ibid.
13. A. Breton, *Surrealism and Painting*, trans. S.W. Taylor (Harper and Row, New York, 1972), p.4.
14. Tickner, 1988, p.29.

Behind the Image
Frances Borzello

For centuries women artists were exceptions in a male profession, so their self-portraits can never be taken for granted. A woman did not have a right to a profession as a man did, not even a woman of talent. Male artists had their problems, too, but a husband was not expected to give up his professional career in the interests of domestic harmony: 'Had Mr. C. permitted me to paint professionally, I should have made a better painter but left to myself instead of improving, I lost what I had brought from Italy of my early studies,' wrote Maria Cosway (1760–1838) in the account of her life which she made for her uncle in 1830.[1] Few male students were forbidden to draw from the nude model as women were for centuries, an unfairness that was accepted with complacency. The Scottish artist Katherine Read (1723–79) went to Rome in 1751 to complete her training as a portrait painter. The abbé Grant, a Scottish Jesuit priest who spent almost fifty years in Rome as the Roman Agent to the Scottish Catholic Mission and who was a supporter of British artists, reported in 1752 that 'Was it not for the restrictions her sex obliges her to be under, I dare safely say she would shine wonderfully in history painting too, but as it is impossible for her to attend public academies or even design or draw from nature, she is determined to confine herself to portraits.'[2] By contrast, the taboos men faced were negligible: for example, the Royal Academy's ban on unmarried men under the age of twenty studying the female nude (the male nude was permitted) had withered away by the end of the nineteenth century. No mention of it was made in the new regulations of 1903 which famously established a life-drawing class for women.

Since every recent history book has stressed how women, until the early twentieth century, were denied the same opportunities as men, how did they find the time, the space, the permission, the psychological daring, to learn and then to practise as artists? Though women artists were far outnumbered by male artists, they were by no means non-existent and many of them prospered. Women artists have played a part in British art for hundreds of years: Levina Teerlinc (1510/20?–76), for example, was employed as a miniature painter in the sixteenth century by four successive monarchs. The proof of their existence faces us in these self-portraits by women who earned the right to the title of artist. However, the experiences behind their self-portraits differ from those of male artists. Although, like men, the women got themselves a training, set themselves up in business, found patrons and frequently enjoyed great success, a woman artist was always seen as out of the ordinary – justifiably so, not just because of her rarity value, but because her relationship with the world of art was not the same as a man's. Firstly, until the end of the nineteenth century, her training was less complete; and secondly, she operated within a set of attitudes about women's suitability to make art that men did not have to deal with.

Until the development of state education systems at the end of the nineteenth century, women could not assume they had any right to train as artists. Before that, the patchy nature of female education ensured that there was little chance of any talent being discovered and, if it did emerge, little chance of it being taken seriously. Money spent on daughters was judiciously measured out: the goal was to make them accomplished enough to attract a husband but not so opinionated that their minds refused to accept the impress of his ideas. The eighteenth-century Italian artist Rosalba Carriera (1675–1757) summed up their stunted opportunities: 'What gives men the advantage over us is their education, the freedom to converse, and the variety of their affairs and acquaintances.'[3] It was no help that painting, with the exception of watercolour, which could be done at a table, or miniatures, where neatness was a prerequisite for success, was not the daintiest of professions. Oil paint was messy, took a long time to dry and could not be carried out in the drawing-room or garden under the watchful eye of polite society. Furthermore, knowledge was necessary to negotiate its chemical mysteries. For the same reasons, sculpture was equally unwelcoming to women.

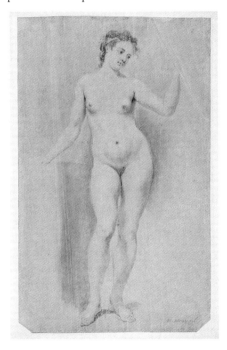

Women artists had nothing like the conveyor belt of apprenticeship or academy that men took for granted, so their training was for centuries a piecemeal affair, put together like a jigsaw and often, as with jigsaws, incomplete. The crucial missing piece in a young woman's artistic education was the opportunity to draw the male nude. This mattered as the profession's highest accolades were reserved for history paintings, a Renaissance ideal of what constituted the most admirable kind of art centring on the artist's ability to paint figures in narrative scenes of heroism, virtue or suffering from history, the classics and the Bible. When training became codified in the seventeenth century, life drawing was joined by perspective and anatomy as the core of the academic curriculum, a curriculum which excluded women.

Although most women before the nineteenth century could not develop the necessary skills for history painting, this was not the case with all. Some determined women found their way round the taboo and learned to paint the body. In the sixteenth century, the Italian Sofonisba Anguissola copied her teacher's painting of the dead half-naked Christ. In England the flower painter Mary Moser (1744–1819) who, in December 1768, alongside Angelica Kauffmann, was one of the two founding female members of the Royal Academy of Arts in London, drew at least one female nude (fig.10). Supportive parents and the confidence of class encouraged the eighteenth-century amateur sculptor Anne Seymour Damer (1749–1828) to become the student of anatomy teacher and surgeon Dr William Cumberland Cruikshank (1745–1800).

10.
Drawing of a female nude
Mary Moser, n.d.
Black and white chalk on paper,
490 x 302mm
(19¼ x 11⅞")
Fitzwilliam Museum, Cambridge

The small number of ambitious women on the Continent from the sixteenth century, and in Britain from the eighteenth, who produced figure paintings mainly chose female-centred subjects in deference to contemporary attitudes about feminine propriety and out of a sense of fitness as to suitable subject matter for women artists. By the mid-nineteenth century, women were beginning to tackle the same genres as men, even the large-scale landscapes previously forbidden them by the awkwardness of sitting alone in public and their ignorance of the scientific knowledge of perspective.

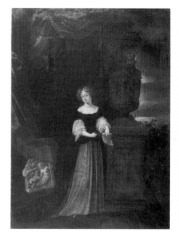

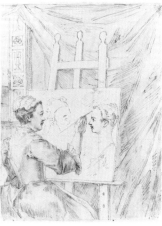

11.
Self-portrait
Anne Killigrew (1660–85)
1680s,
Oil on canvas,
743 x 794mm (29¼ x 31¼")
R.J.G. Berkeley,
Berkeley Castle

12.
Lady Burlington at her easel in her Garden Room
Dorothy Savile, Countess of Burlington (1699–1758)
William Kent, *c*.1740
Pen and pencil,
231 x 181mm (9⅛ x 7⅛")
Devonshire Collection,
Chatsworth

Until the eighteenth century a woman's best chance for the discovery and development of talent was to be the daughter of an artist with access to a workshop or a wealthy young woman with a sympathetic family who could provide the means to decent tuition. Lessons which veered towards the superficial ensured that there was only a limited amount of crossover from amateur to professional but some women managed to make the leap. In seventeenth-century England, Mary Beale made the artistic transition from country clergyman's daughter, probably first taught to paint by her amateur artist father, to the head of a London portrait studio.

More common was an intermediate breed of artist, the committed upper-class amateur. This quintessentially female inhabitant of the art world is symbolised by the amateur poet and painter Anne Killigrew, a member of the court of Charles II. Her self-portrait of the 1680s, in which she shows herself doubly talented, with poem in hand and in a setting of draperies, classical reliefs and urn that typifies the baroque trappings of the period, is hardly the product of the kind of amateur who would modestly shield her work with her arm when anyone entered the room (fig.11). Most amateurs worked in pencil, watercolours and coloured chalks. Amateurs who worked in oil, such as Anne Killigrew and Dorothy Savile, Countess of Burlington, who was sketched around 1740 by her teacher, the architect and landscape designer William Kent (1685?–1748) as she worked on her self-portrait with her daughter in her garden room studio (fig.12), were unusual. Because these were 'ladies' as well as artists, their work was assessed with gallantry and in the tones of seriousness reserved for professionals. Anne Damer was a good sculptor, but Horace Walpole's view in *Anecdotes of Painting in England* (1762–71) that her terracotta model of a dog rivalled one in marble by Gian Lorenzo Bernini (1598–1680) in the Royal Collection is like comparing cider with champagne.

Although the admission of women to art schools in the second half of the nineteenth century is traditionally seen as the decisive event that gave them educational equality, a general encouragement for women existed as early as the eighteenth century, when many more women outside the artist's daughter/well-born amateur nexus went into the profession. A key factor in encouraging women to take up art was the culture of accomplishment, which reached its peak in the second half of the eighteenth century; the fact that much of the art produced by amateurs was second rate was balanced by the fact that women making art became a common sight in civilised society. Secondly, women who wanted to paint could call up the roll of female painters in their support: the funeral oration in Paris in 1712 for the painter Elisabeth-Sophie Chéron (1648–1711) placed her in a line headed by Lavinia Fontana and the Anguissola sisters. Thirdly, the fame of Rosalba Carriera's portraits, publicised in Britain through her likenesses of the Grand Tourists in Italy, resulted in a rash of copycat female pastel portraitists, amateur as well as professional. In 1766, Angelica Kauffmann brought the latest neoclassical ideas to London in her portfolio. Britain had always relied on immigrant artists such as Hans Holbein the Younger (1497/8–1543) in the sixteenth century and Sir Anthony van Dyck in the seventeenth to show them the way to greater things. With Angelica Kauffmann's visit came the women's very own inspiration. Her scenes from classical history were sometimes mocked for the femininity of her male figures, but no one argued with her influential position in the art world.

One by one, in the final decades of the nineteenth century, the doors to the art schools gave way before the women's pushing hands (fig.13). Even then, they sometimes had to supplement their training. At the age of thirteen, Laura Knight, née Johnson, was sent to the Nottingham School of Art to shape her talent into a marketable profession as a teacher. Irritated by the school's attitude to its women students (no life drawing and an assumption that they were less serious than the men), she attached herself to Harold Knight (1874–1961), an older and more artistically advanced student whom she later married, and set out on the successful career which culminated in her election to the Royal Academy in 1936.

Academies were not the only way to learn. Men had always travelled to study famous works of art and gradually women began to follow. After 1750 several women, including Katherine Read (from 1751–3), Angelica Kauffmann (1763–5) and Anne Forbes (1768–71), went to Rome, then the centre of the art world as Paris was to become a century later. There they could see the fabled classical statues that set the standard for the perfect human form and the revered art of the sixteenth and seventeenth centuries. Best of all, they could meet the wealthy British Grand Tourists, finishing their education and sowing their wild oats if they were young men, enjoying the sights if they were older. These were the people they hoped would form their client base on their return to England. A hundred years later, young women from all over the world went off to Paris, a city ready to offer them education in its studios. Free to live alone or be with friends, free to take themselves seriously, free to admit their competitiveness with the male students and with each other, their recollections reveal their conviction that artistic honours were theirs to claim. Short of money in Paris in the twentieth century's first decade, Gwen John hired herself out as a nude model and found herself the object of her employers' desires. She returned the sculptor Auguste Rodin's (1840–1917) interest in her with a love that far outlasted his. In these years of finding herself and her artistic direction, Gwen John did several sketches of herself naked in her Parisian room (fig.14; see p.26). In fact, the nude self-portrait was a feature of female self-portraiture at this time: the work of the German artist Paula Modersohn-Becker (1876–1907) is another example of a development which sums up the women's curiosity about themselves in this brave new world of self-discovery and artistic opportunities.

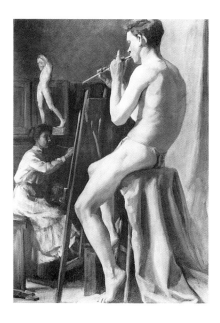

13.
A Life Class
Thomas Gillott, 1912
Oil on canvas,
750 x 550mm (29½ x 21⅝")
Nottingham City Museums and Galleries, Castle Museum and Art Gallery

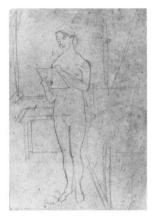

14.
Self-portrait, Nude Sketching
Gwen John (1876–1939),
1908–9
Pencil, 235 x 165mm (9¼ x 6½")
National Museum of Wales

When it came to setting up in business, women had to operate within the demands of family life and feminine propriety. Mary Beale in the seventeenth century was lucky: hers was a true family business, a painting workshop which she headed with the practical support of her husband and children. While her husband ran her studio, kept the accounts and, fascinated by such matters as the drying properties of various oils and the chemistry of colours, took care of the technical side, her sons helped in the preparation and underpainting of her canvases. As well as using members of their family to help out, women artists took students or apprentices, partly as an extra pair of hands, partly as an extra income. Two of Mary Beale's three apprentices were young women. One, Kate Trioche, has faded completely except for her name and an unfinished portrait that is thought to show her (fig.15). The other, Sarah Hoadley, followed in her teacher's footsteps and for a period worked as a portrait painter.

Professionalism was necessary for success. In October 1766, two months after settling in London, Angelica Kauffmann wrote to her father: 'I have four rooms, one in which I paint, the other where I set up my finished paintings as is here the custom, [so that] the people [can] come into the house to sit – to visit me – or to see my work; I could not possibly receive people in a poorly furnished house.' Lack of organisation was death to any portrait practice. The Scottish artist Anne Forbes (1745–1834), who spent the winter of 1772–3 trying to establish a portrait practice in London, wrote home to Edinburgh that she had thirteen paintings in a state of incompletion due to the constant damp weather

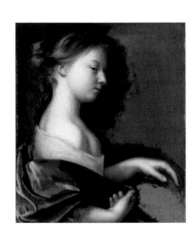

15.
Portrait of a Young Girl
Kate Trioche
Mary Beale, *c*.1681
Oil on canvas,
535 x 460mm (21⅛ x 18⅛")
Tate, London

which prevented them from drying. Good health was also important in keeping the production line going. Anne Forbes's mother compared her daughter's poor health with that of Angelica Kauffmann 'who added to her great facility has such a constitution that she is able to work from 5 in the Morning till sunset in Summer and during the whole daylight in Winter, whereas Anne can not rise till eight or fall to work till ten, nor will she attempt it for any consideration, sleeping her only support as well as luxury.'[4] Women's frailty was often cited by men as a barrier to their achievements. Aware of this, Elizabeth Thompson (later Lady Butler) vowed in the 1860s not to be categorised as a sickly female: 'I was never ill, nor rather, I never allowed myself to be ill, or to have headaches and migraines to which so many girls in those days yielded obeisance.' Their professionalism started early. Before the twentieth century gave them a complete academic structure, women had to work harder than men to create a rigorous training for themselves. Elizabeth Thompson could not get all the training she considered necessary at the Female School of Art in South Kensington and took an extra-curricular class to study what she called the 'undraped' female model. Still feeling ill-prepared to launch her career at the conclusion of her studies, she went to Italy with her family in 1869 to study with the academic draughtsman Giuseppe Bellucci (1827–82). Her self-portrait (see p.43) is thought to have been produced at this time, when she was drilled in drawing 'more severely than I could have been drilled in England'.[5]

It was particularly important for women to be seen to conduct themselves impeccably if they were to be admitted into intimacy with their upper-class female clients. This was not as simple as it sounds. The fashionable world was intrigued at the idea of women artists alone in rooms with men, going about and selling their wares, perhaps drawing nude male models, and was quick to create gossip about them. Angelica Kauffmann was a favourite target in her London years. Rumoured to be intimate with the celebrated painter Sir Joshua Reynolds, doyen of the London art world and the Royal Academy's first president, she figured in a painted scandal when she was alleged to be the half-nude woman in the corner of the Irish artist Nathaniel Hone's (1718–84) satirical portrait of Reynolds. Twenty years after her death, it was still a matter of fascination as to whether she had drawn from the male nude model. An aged ex-Royal Academy model told an interviewer in 1827 that 'he only exposed his arms, shoulders and legs, and that her father, who was also an artist and likewise an exhibitor at the Royal Academy, was always present'.[6] It says much for Kauffmann's professionalism that she survived all such attacks and remained a respected member of the artistic community.

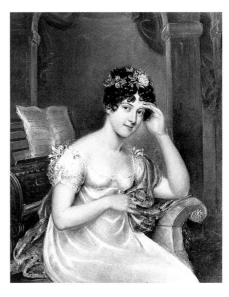

16.
Self-portrait
Rolinda Sharples
(1793–1838), *c.*1814
Oil on panel,
311 x 248mm (12¼ x 9¾")
Bristol Museum and Art Gallery

Finding commissions was difficult for women, for whom anything approaching self-advertisement was thought to be unfeminine. Courts provided a haven for artists in the sixteenth and seventeenth centuries but as the open market became increasingly important, women had to find their own clients. Portraiture was the only kind of art the British wanted, and by the eighteenth century competition among painters was politely cut-throat. Anne Forbes and her family waited for clients to come by, as her mother recorded: 'Mrs Pelham has at last favoured us with a call in, but no more, she is sitting to Sir Joshua, Miss Angelica and Dance.'[7] Names and addresses of exhibitors were included in catalogues but this brought no guarantee of clients knocking on the studio door: 'all the world was at the exhibition and in the catalogue every artist's name and place of abode was mark'd so if any one had been so minded to do her service she was easy to be found,' wrote Mrs Forbes in a lament about her daughter's difficulties in breaking into the fashionable world despite her years in Rome among the British Grand Tourists.[8]

An artist could only stop worrying when she had a circle of patrons to rely on. For two decades women and their children came to Katherine Read's studio in London's West End, a stopping place on the fashionable morning walk, to have their portraits made in pastel. The young Fanny Burney (1752–1840), later to become a famous novelist, recorded being taken there by her mother in her diary of 1774. In Bristol in the early nineteenth century, Rolinda Sharples made a name as the chronicler of local places and events, a kind of artistic Jane Austen (fig.16). To become known for a reliable product was of immense help in terms of reputation and income. In 1874, Elizabeth Thompson attracted so much attention with *The Roll Call*, the first of her large battle paintings, that Queen Victoria demanded it be brought for her to view at Windsor Castle. In the early twentieth century, the name of Laura Knight became synonymous with paintings of female circus and ballet performers.

There seems little point in projecting contemporary feminist thoughts and feelings on to the women artists of the past. In fact, it is their acceptance of the art world's rules and their determination to negotiate their way around them that makes them so fascinating a study. They obviously understood the attitudes they faced – 'Tis true we are all but strangers in this world, and I ought not to think myself more so than others, but my unlucky sex lays me under inconveniences which cause these reflections,' wrote Katherine Read – but they seem to have regarded them as no more than occupational hazards.[9] This refusal to blame their sex for their difficulties continued into the twentieth century, when some very strange views about women's abilities (that their creativity went into motherhood), commitment (that creativity automatically waned with marriage) and nature (that they lacked the competitive streak) plus the conviction that talent would rise to the surface like cream whatever the artist's circumstances, served to undermine their official equality. Their private writings show that many women were aware of the flaws in these theories, but in public they denied that their gender had any bearing on their progress through the art world. Dame Barbara Hepworth was one who understood the public's tendency to equate female with second rate. In an attempt to downplay the issue of her gender, she published a pictorial autobiography in 1969 to show how in her case family and work coexisted as seamlessly as they did for men.

Looking at women solely in terms of the obstacles they faced obscures the fact that there were many successful artists and there were many satisfactions in being an artist, including status, income, self-fulfilment and, no doubt for some, the secret pleasure of standing out from the crowd. Rolinda Sharples' supportive mother appreciated the advantages for a woman of working in an unusual profession in the early nineteenth century: 'Exercising it as a profession she views it as attended with every kind of advantage. The employment itself is a positive pleasure; it produces many articles of utility and luxury that otherwise would be regarded as extravagance; the persons she draws entertain her whilst sitting, become her friends and continue to be so, ever after meeting her with smiling countenances and kind greetings.'[10]

Artists historically have been seen as male, beret-crowned individuals with a model on each arm and one left exhausted on the studio couch. There is no comparable stereotype of a woman artist. The two most common images are the amateur who dabbles and does not work for money and the bohemian, a creature of escaping hairpins and untidy dress, a product of the late nineteenth century. Both are figures of fun. Just as the stereotype of the artist is male, so is the self-portrait. Most people know about Van Gogh's self-portrait with a bandage over his mutilated ear, or the stream of self-portraits from Rembrandt's hand, chronicling his life from youth to inscrutable age. And yet women have produced them, too. It is one of art history's best-kept secrets. In the sixteenth century Sofonisba Anguissola made over twenty self-portraits to satisfy the curiosity of her Italian and Spanish patrons about that rarity, a woman artist. In the 1920s the Mexican Frida Kahlo (1907–54) began to turn her whole life into a visual diary. Her paintings record her crippling accident as an adolescent, her miscarriages, her love for the muralist Diego Rivera (1886–1957) and her desperation when he rejected her.

Although it is possible for a self-portrait to be little more than a transcription of what the artist sees in the mirror, most women settling down to paint themselves give serious consideration to what they want to put on canvas. As with autobiography, the truth that is told, the picture that is presented, is controlled by the artist. But it is also affected by what is permitted to her by the demands of the day regarding artistic conventions and feminine behaviour.

Until the twentieth century put its seal of approval on self-revelation, women had to think carefully about how they spoke about themselves in their self-portraits. To begin with, they had to align the activity of the professional with the passive role awarded them by art. Until the nineteenth century, women in portraits are rarely active. They sit, read, sew or hold a pet or a child. The women who do things are servants – think of the sweepers and shopkeepers of seventeenth-century Dutch paintings. The task for a woman was to paint herself engaged in an activity without looking masculine or lower class. Women also had to reconcile their depiction of their professionalism with society's expectations of femininity. Smudges on the nose, weary rings under the eyes and clothes daubed with paint were for the studio and not the canvas. Women presumably did get paint all over themselves, but until the end of the nineteenth century, there is never a hint of it in their self-portraits. Although the French portraitist Elisabeth-Louise Vigée Le Brun (1755–1842) describes in her *Mémoires* (published 1835–7) how she sat on her palette without noticing the mess on her dress, this example of artistic concentration was not one to be made visible at a time when female charm and elegance were at a premium. The period introduced informal male self-portraits of the artists looking less than imposing – Chardin with eye shade (fig. 3; see p.12), Hogarth at his easel, wearing a velvet cap over his shaven head – but the time had not come for their female counterpart to show herself as less than enchanting in her many self-portraits.

Always inventive, women adapted male self-portrait patterns for their own use. One such pattern was the artist holding evidence of expertise in the form of his drawing of the nude model. Though propriety and in most cases fact prevented women from borrowing this format, they managed to suggest a similar artistic grounding as early as the sixteenth century when Lavinia Fontana painted herself surrounded by small casts, a modest way to display her knowledge of the male nude (fig.17).

Some self-portrait patterns were shared with male artists. Like their male counterparts women painted themselves as successful and elegant members of society, proud of their profession. Like the male artists they painted manifesto self-portraits which revealed their artistic allegiance. These could be as straightforward as Paule Vézelay's self-portrait of *c*.1927–9, painted in a cubist manner (see p.65), or as elaborate as Angelica Kauffmann's version of the myth of Zeuxis painting Helen of Troy, a subject which expresses her belief that perfection can only be found in art and not in the individual object. In *Zeuxis Selecting*

17.
Self-portrait with Small Statues
Lavinia Fontana
(1552–1614), 1579
Oil on copper,
diameter 157mm (6⅛")
Galleria degli Uffizi,
Corridoio Vasariano

Models for His Painting of Helen of Troy (*c.*1778; Annmary Brown Memorial Collection, Providence) she ingeniously pushes the myth in the direction of self-portraiture by giving her own features to one of the five women from whom Zeuxis constructs his composite of perfection and by having her take up Zeuxis' paintbrush.

Certain self-portrait patterns became the property of women. A female portrait format which emerged in the eighteenth century – the depiction of the accomplished lady amateur with a crayon under her languid hand instead of a dog – was borrowed by some professionals. Angelica Kauffmann, a working artist – in other words, in trade – disguises herself as a lady amateur, one hand resting lightly on a portfolio, the other modestly pointing towards herself as the author (see p.37). Self-portraits showing the artist as a musician, a theme that Sofonisba Anguissola first employed in the sixteenth century to display her double talents, recur down the centuries. A number of female self-portraits involve helpers in the artist's family. Mary Beale painted herself holding her portrait of the sons who later prepared her canvases (see p.35). Over 200 years later, Lallie Charles photographed herself with her sisters Rita and Beaulah Martin who helped in her studio (see p.47).

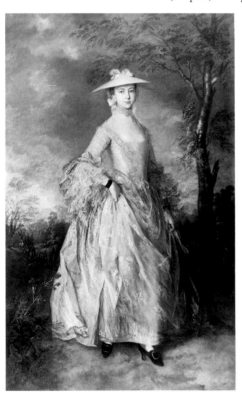

18.
Mary, Countess Howe
Thomas Gainsborough, *c.*1760
Oil on canvas,
2440 x 1524mm (96 x 60")
Kenwood, The Iveagh Bequest

Self-portraits are a way to understand women's experiences and ingenuity in negotiating the art world of their day. As their circumstances changed, so did their self-portraits. Milly Childers' confident view of herself (see p.45) is typical of a whole batch of dynamic self-portraits from ambitious women at the turn of the twentieth century who felt that entry into art school would be their making. Indifferent to her audience, her huge palette is a professional barrier that forbids us to patronise her in any way.

Like autobiography, self-portraits demand to be read. Some clues are obvious: the insignia of the St John's Ambulance Brigade, which Anna Zinkeisen wears as a bracelet, is a touch of patriotism in a painting made in the midst of World War II (see p.85). Others are artistic, a matter of pose, influence or style. Gwen John was not a large woman and yet it is clear from her decision to make her body touch each side of the canvas that she wanted to present herself as substantial and determined (see p.49). The fact that Ann Mary Newton seems firmly protective of her work (see p.41) while Angelica Kauffmann seems diffident, is to do with Newton's decision to pose away from us and Kauffmann's towards us. Anna Zinkeisen's dashingly placed arm echoes one of the most glamorous portraits in English art, Thomas Gainsborough's Mary, Countess Howe (fig.18), surely a knowing reference on the part of this stylish artist.

The publication of feminist analyses of around 1970 arguably did as much for the cause of women artists as had their entry into art schools in the previous century. Not only did they begin the interest in women artists of the past of which this book is a descendant, but their political arm examined the unfairnesses of the official art world, which for centuries had redirected institutional sexism on to innate female characteristics. A resulting benefit to female students was that many developed a new self-confidence. No longer demanding to be seen as artists first and women second, they drew from their experiences as women in order to create work which they sent into the sacred male art gallery space.

In recent years there has been an expansion in what a self-portrait can present and women can take much credit for this. The feminist revolution gave women permission to value their own lives and feelings and ideas as highly as men did theirs, and though the results often caused outrage, particularly when taboo subjects such as menstruation appeared in women artists' works, they were impossible to ignore. This new subject matter, the artistic arm of the feminist slogan that the personal is the political, has led to the most exciting developments in self-portraiture today: the extended self-portrait, an elaborate idea expressed through the self. Jenny Saville has visualised her concern about the tyranny wielded over women by the fantasy of the perfect body in a series of larger-than-life-size nudes overlain with contour lines, words, and the kind of marks made by plastic surgeons in preparation for their cuts. Her innovation was to use her own distorted and enlarged nude body (fig.19). In 1995, Mona Hatoum (b.1952) made a video of a medical probe's journey into her orifices, a contemporary version of the nude self-portraits of the century's start. Far from dead, the self-portrait is continually reinventing itself and it is women who lead the way in its exciting extension into the realm of ideas.

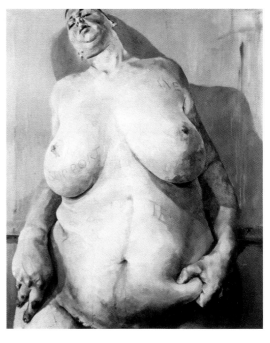

19.
Branded
Jenny Saville,
(b.1970), 1992
Oil on canvas,
2135 x 1830mm
(84 x 72")
The Saatchi Gallery, London

Notes

1. Autograph letter to William Cosway, 24 May 1830, National Art Library, Victoria and Albert Museum.
2. Lady Victoria Manners, 'Catherine Read: The English Rosalba', the *Connoisseur*, vol.88 (1931) p.380.
3. C. Harrison, P. Wood, J. Gaiger, *Art in Theory 1648–1815* (Oxford, 2000), p.315.

4. Forbes Letters 1772–3, National Library of Scotland, Edinburgh, f.124v.
5. This and previous two quotes from *Lady Elisabeth Butler (formerly Thompson), An Autobiography*, (London, 1922), pp.20; 46; 66.
6. John Thomas Smith, *Nollekens and His Times*, 2 vols. (London, 1828), vol.1, p.69.

7. Forbes, f.139r.
8. Forbes, f.138v.
9. Manners, op. cit., p.380.
10. Katharine McCook Knox, *The Sharples* (New Haven, 1930), p.52.

MIRROR
MIRROR

Mary Beale (1633–99)
*c.*1665
Oil on canvas, 1092 x 876mm (43 x 34½")
National Portrait Gallery, London (NPG 1687)

Born Mary Cradock, the daughter of a Puritan Suffolk clergyman, Mary Beale was one of the very few women artists working in England during the seventeenth century and has been called the first truly professional female artist in Britain.

Like Angelica Kauffmann (see pp.36–7), Mary Beale's mother died when she was young (about ten years old). Her father, who knew the artist Robert Walker (1599–1658), introduced her to painting. In 1652 she married Charles Beale, who, like her father, was also an amateur painter. Around 1654 they were in London, where Mary embarked on a semi-professional career as a portrait painter; in 1658 she is mentioned in Sir William Sanderson's *Graphice or, The Use of the Pen and Pensil, in Designing, Drawing, and Painting…* Her first son, Bartholomew, was baptised at St Paul's, Covent Garden, in 1656, and her second son, Charles, who later became a miniature painter, was born in 1660.

In this painting she affirms her position as an artist by showing us a palette hanging on the wall behind her, and her status as a portrait painter and mother – her right hand rests on a canvas portraying her sons. Self-portraits are rare during this period, so it is interesting to note that of Anne Killigrew (fig.11; see p.24), described by Dryden as 'Excellent in the two Sister-Arts of Poesie and Painting'. Like Mary Beale's it is an interesting variation on a conventional late-seventeenth-century image.

In 1670 Mary established a studio in Pall Mall and became friends with Sir Peter Lely, court painter to Charles II. Her husband – who might perhaps be called a 'new man' before his time – was her assistant, mixing paint and keeping the 'notebooks' containing details of her accounts and sittings. His notebook of 1677 (in the Bodleian Library) details a busy year: eighty-three commissions yielding earnings of £429. Following Lely's death in 1680, his style of portraiture (and Mary's by imitation) became outmoded. Charles's notebook of 1681 (in the National Portrait Gallery's collection) refers to the family's reduced financial circumstances, '… we had but only 2s.6d. left us in the house against Easter'. In these notebooks, Charles Beale often refers to his wife as 'Dearest Heart'. Mary Beale worked until her death at the age of sixty-six and is buried in St James's, Piccadilly. Her husband died in 1705.

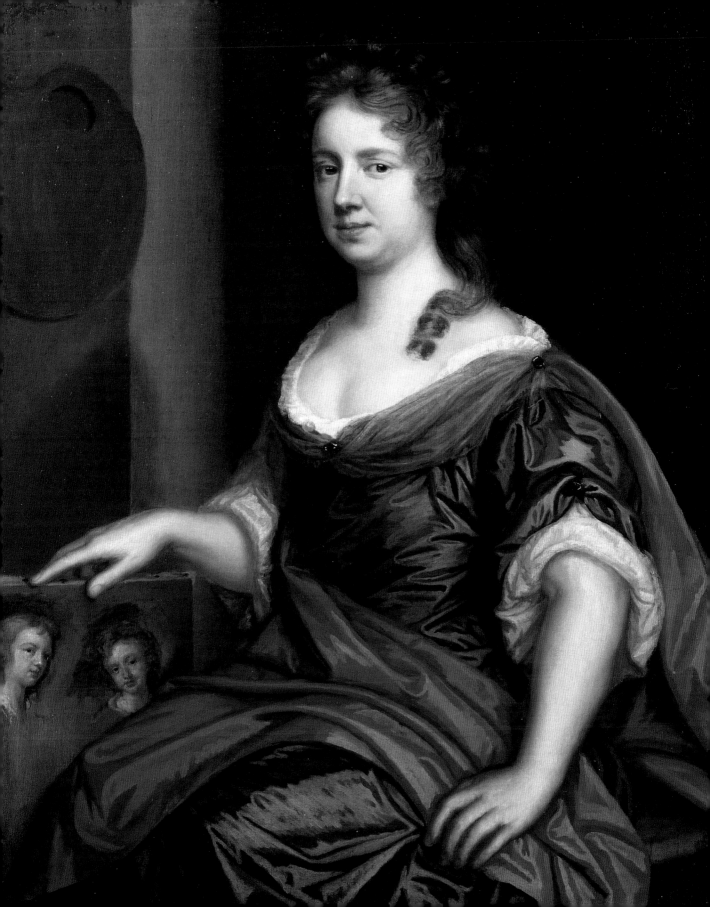

Angelica Kauffmann (1741–1807)
*c.*1770–5
Oil on canvas, 737 x 610mm (29 x 24")
National Portrait Gallery, London (NPG 430)

Angelica Kauffmann was born in Switzerland. She was equally talented as a musician and as an artist. Her mother died when she was sixteen and her father (also an artist) taught her and travelled with her to Italy, where she was permitted to copy paintings in a private room in the Uffizi. In her book *The Obstacle Race: The fortunes of women painters and their work* (1979) Germaine Greer called her a 'marvellous hybrid: free from the overwhelming influence of any single master'.

In 1762 Kauffmann was accepted as a member of the Accademia del Disegno, Florence, and in 1763 she went to Rome, where she became friends with the German historian and art critic Johann Winckelmann (1717–68), making her name with her portrait of him in 1764. She came to London in 1766 and two years later became a founder member of the Royal Academy of Arts (the only other female member was Mary Moser). Kauffmann painted Sir Joshua Reynolds in 1767 and was described by the contemporary writer James Boswell as 'musician, paintress, modest, amiable'. Her work was popular and her decorative history pieces were widely engraved and used in the manufacture of objets d'art. She painted many self-portraits (see p.10), the first at the age of just thirteen, and used herself as the protagonist in her allegorical works, for example as 'Design', as 'Imitation', and in the painting *Self-portrait in the Character of Painting Embraced by Poetry* (1782; Kenwood, The Iveagh Bequest). In 1781 she married the artist Antonio Zucchi (1726–95; her first marriage was a failure – to a bigamist count). Zucchi, a less distinguished painter, was an ideal husband – he could assume the role of male chaperone and mediator – and she returned to Italy with him and her father, who died in 1782. In 1785 she painted a history painting for Catherine the Great, Empress of Russia, and in 1787 she came back to Rome when she was invited to contribute her self-portrait to the prestigious Medici collection of self-portraits in the Uffizi. In that same year she became friends with the great German poet Goethe (1749–1832).

In this self-portrait Kauffmann points to herself whilst looking at us and balancing her drawing book under her right hand, which is poised ready to draw with her pastel. The latter is held firmly in a 'porte-crayon', which allowed more flexibility of movement, and therefore more fluid and gestural marks, by adding length to the pastel stick. (At this time pastels would have been quite stumpy and fragile as they were handmade from pure pigment and gum arabic.) The painting is bathed in a warm soft light. Kauffmann's skin appears translucent and her clothing echoes the folds and curls of her tumbling hair. Distinctly feminine and seductive, the work reinforces her determination as a woman artist rather than merely showing off her skills. Kauffmann presents herself and the tools of her trade as an aesthetic statement.

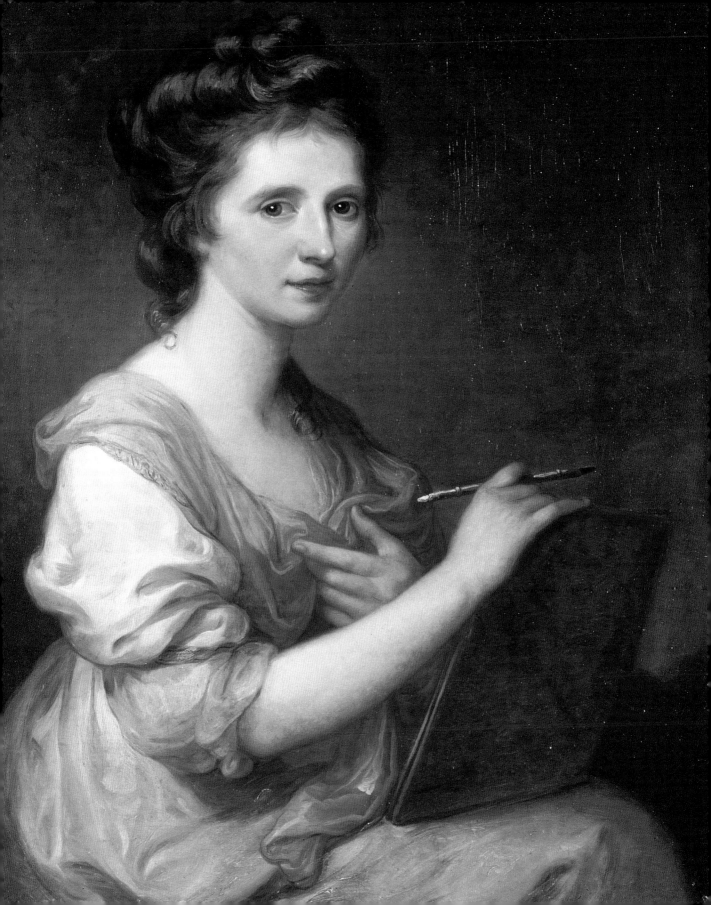

Attributed to **Mary Ann Flaxman** (1768–1833)
*c.*1820
Watercolour on ivory, actual size 70 x 54mm (2¾ x 2⅛")
National Portrait Gallery, London (NPG 1715)

This miniature is thought to be by Mary Ann Flaxman, the sister of the well-known sculptor John Flaxman (1755–1826), who was appointed Professor of Sculpture in 1810 to the Royal Academy Schools. Mary Ann lived for a while with her brother, who was renowned for his generosity: his sister-in-law also lived with them and both women practised as amateur painters. Mary Ann exhibited at the Royal Academy of Arts between 1786 and 1819, showing portraits and genre pictures with titles such as *Ferdinand and Miranda Playing Chess* (1789), *Sappho* (1810) and *Maternal Piety* (1819). There are also references to other works by her in the Royal Academy lists of exhibitors, including drawings, designs after poems and a portrait in wax from 1789.

John Flaxman senior originally came from York and had a business making plaster casts and models, often of antique subjects. His shop was first in New Street, Covent Garden, and he then moved to larger premises on the Strand. Mary Ann must have enjoyed coming into contact with her father's famous customers, who included the sculptors Louis François Roubiliac (1702–62) and Peter Scheemakers (1691–1781) and the industrialist Josiah Wedgwood (1730–95). John Flaxman junior went to the Royal Academy Schools in 1769 and in *c.*1772 he produced a charming wax portrait of his 4-year-old sister sitting in a chair, her foot balanced on a mug, holding and caressing her doll (now in the Victoria and Albert Museum, London). It is a piece of perfect observation with delicate touches within the rendering of the hair, the ruched lace bonnet and the drapery folds of her dress. This wax was probably that exhibited at the Royal Academy as *Figure of a Child* in 1772.

Little is known of Mary Ann Flaxman. Her self-portrait, carefully built up with stippled paint, was bought for the National Portrait Gallery in 1913. It depicts a woman with an expression of sweet resignation, calm, with a hint of a smile and a dimple. She is well dressed, the curly fringe peeping out from under her lacy cap is the only suggestion of female coquetry.

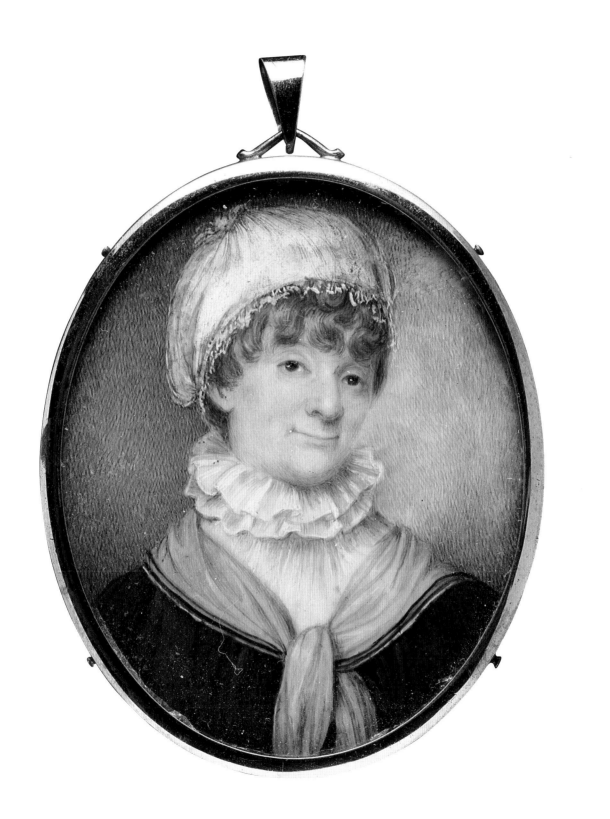

Ann Mary Newton (1832–66)
Exhibited Royal Academy, 1863
Oil on canvas, 610 x 521mm (24 x 20½")
National Portrait Gallery, London (NPG 977)

Ann Mary Newton was born in Rome where her father, the painter Joseph Severn (1793–1879), taught her to draw, encouraging her to copy engravings by Albrecht Dürer, Michelangelo and Raphael. In England she studied with George Richmond (1809–96) who lent her some of his portraits to copy, and she was so talented at this that he employed her for that purpose.

Aged twenty-three Ann Mary went to Paris to study with Ary Scheffer (1795–1858), and whilst there she painted a watercolour of the Countess of Elgin. The success of this work led to further commissions and eventually a portrait practice in London. At the age of twenty-six, she had displaced her father as the main breadwinner. She painted various portraits and produced drawings for Queen Victoria and members of the royal family, and exhibited at the Royal Academy in 1852, 1855 and 1856. In 1861 she married Sir Charles Newton (1816–94), who, in a peculiar type of 'bargain', offered her father the post he was relinquishing as British Consul in Rome – Charles wished to resume working as an archaeologist and Keeper of Classical Antiquities at the British Museum. Ann Mary devoted the rest of her life to drawing the antiquities in that collection for her husband's books and lectures, and accompanying him on his excavations in Greece and Asia Minor. She died of measles on 2 January 1866.

This rather severe, accomplished and beautiful work shows the artist in a difficult contrapposto pose, her hands clasped over the top of her portfolio and her eyes fixed on us. Her parted hair is adorned with a simple red band, the colour of which is picked up by the bows on the folio and hinted at on her lips and the gem at the centre of her Victorian bracelet. Two rows of big jet beads surround her neck, their size and colour echoed in her eyes. The feigned oval in the background echoes the shape of her curved brow. Her dress, with its delicate gold embroidery, is rendered by a glaze of blue over red, producing a beautiful colour. The focus of our attention is directed to the light sources in the painting: her face, hands and the small piece of paper protruding from her folio, the symbol of her work. The painting was exhibited at the Royal Academy in 1863, and *The Times* critic commented that it was indicative of the artist's ambition that she showed herself as an artist, not just a pretty face. Ann Mary's obituary in the same newspaper on 23 January, three years later, claimed 'After her marriage Mrs Newton became even a more devoted and conscientious labourer in her art than before. Following her husband's studies with the double interest of a devoted wife and an enthusiastic artist.' (Quoted in D. Cherry, *Painting Women: Victorian women artists*, 1993, p.40.)

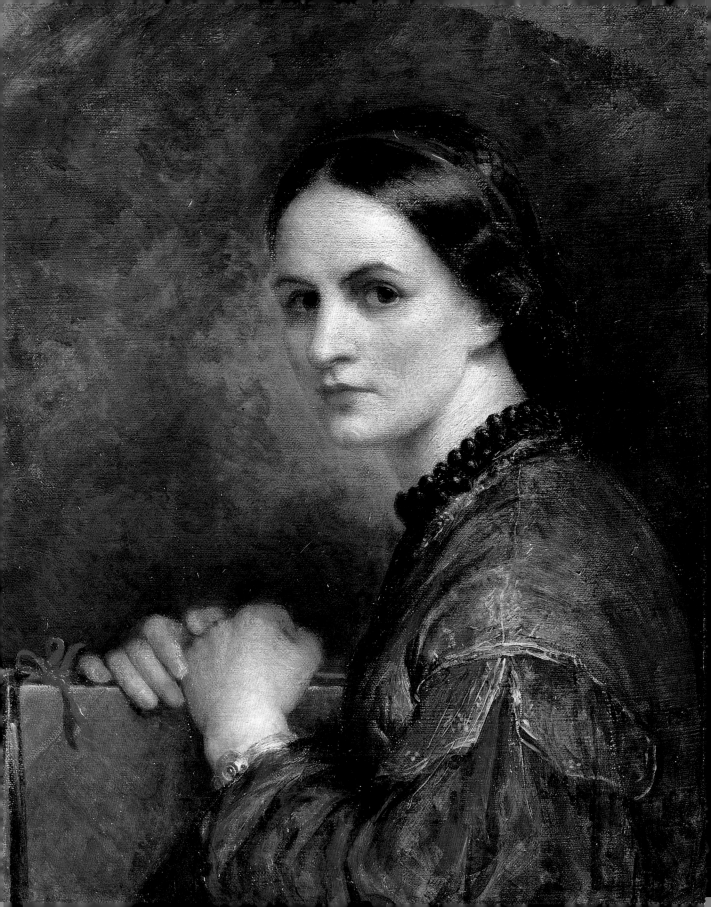

Elizabeth, Lady Butler (1846–1933)
1869
Oil on card, 219 x 181mm (8⅝ x 7⅛")
National Portrait Gallery, London (NPG 5314)

Born in Switzerland of British parents, Elizabeth (née Thompson), who was known as Mimi, and her sister Alice (1847–1922), later the poet Alice Meynell, had a relaxed and rather bohemian education in Italy.

From 1866 to 1870 Mimi attended the Female School of Art, South Kensington, where Kate Greenaway also studied. During this time she met both Sir John Everett Millais (1829–96) and John Ruskin (1819–1900), and in the summer of 1869 she studied figure drawing in Florence. In 1872 she sketched the army during autumn manoeuvres in the New Forest and in 1874, aged twenty-eight, she became instantly famous when she exhibited *The Roll Call* at the Royal Academy. Originally commissioned and paid for by the Manchester industrialist Charles Galloway, the painting so impressed Queen Victoria that she bought it from him. He retained the copyright, which he subsequently sold for £1,200. The work was so popular that a policeman was detailed to stand by it in order to control the enthusiastic crowds. William Holman Hunt (1827–1910) wrote: 'It touched the nation's heart as few pictures have ever done.' That year she visited Paris and met the painter Jean-Léon Gérôme (1824–1904). Her connection with the army deepened when in 1877 she married Major William Butler, with whom she had six children. Lady Butler was never invited to become a Royal Academician, although in 1879 she was short-listed with Sir Hubert von Herkomer (1849–1914), losing to him by two votes. She painted military works all her life and travelled widely with her husband, including two trips to Egypt in 1885 and 1890 to 1893. They also visited the Holy Land in April 1891. Lady Butler was an enthusiastic traveller:

> What a treat … it was to rove about in the reality of the true East, to meet beauty of form and colour and light and shade and movement wherever one's eyes turned, without being brought up with a nasty jar by some modern hideosity or other.
> (E. Butler, *From Sketch-Book and Diary,* 1909, p.37)

This small, delicate oval painting, thought to have been produced when the artist studied in Florence under Giuseppe Bellucci, is a modest self-assessment, concise and retiring, captivating the viewer with its warm background.

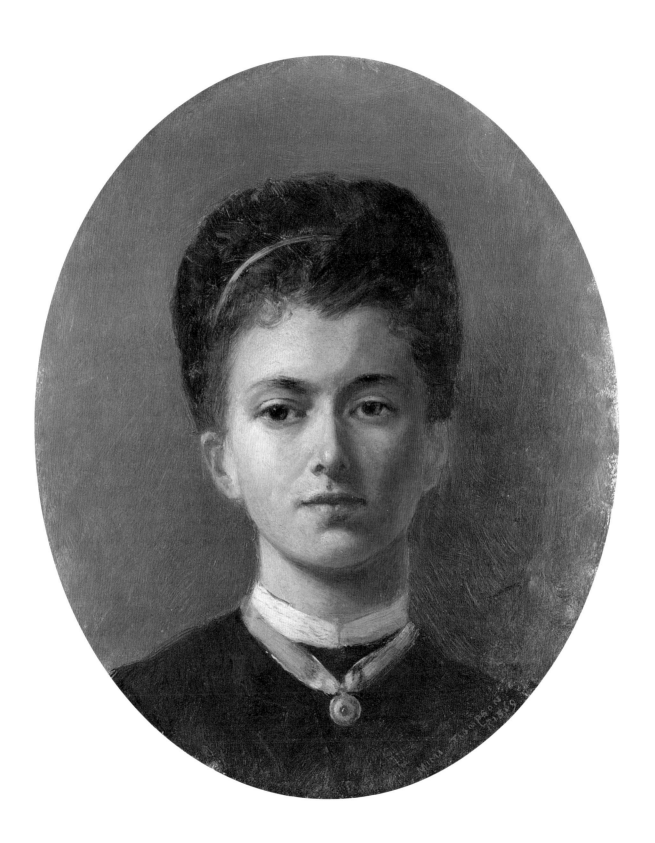

Milly Childers (d.1922; active 1888–1921)
1889
Oil on canvas, 920 x 680mm (36¼ x 26¾")
Leeds Museums and Galleries (City Art Gallery)

Little is known about Milly Childers' artistic training, but she first exhibited a painting at the Royal Society of British Artists in 1890. Her portrait of her father, Hugh Culling Eardley Childers (1827–96), who was MP for Pontefract (1860–85), Chancellor of the Exchequer (1882–5) and Home Secretary in Gladstone's cabinet (1886), is in the collection of the National Portrait Gallery. It portrays him in a grey suit and top hat, relaxing and reading in a sunny garden in Menton, France, in 1891, a year before he retired. The surrounding garden is a vibrant green, and this strength of colour is not unlike that displayed in her self-portrait.

In this confident work Childers is wearing a bright-red painting smock that grabs our attention. She has also arranged her colours on the palette from light to dark in the manner demonstrated by William Hogarth (1697–1764) in his self-portrait in the National Portrait Gallery.

With its dramatic presentation and its skilful references to the art of the past, this painting testifies to the presence and identity of women as producers of culture and meaning in nineteenth-century Britain. The woman's gaze is direct and unflinching, a steady regard of those who are watching her.
(D. Cherry, *Painting Women: Victorian women artists*, 1993)

The focus is on her in the centre of the canvas, the dark background reinforcing the glow of light on her partially turned head, as she surveys us. Her signature is clearly inscribed in black, at the bottom left-hand corner of the work, as in the portrait of her father. There is no ornamentation, only the clever conceit of spread brushes and flat palette – perhaps invoking a painterly fan?

Once her father had retired, Childers travelled with him in England and France, producing landscapes and church interiors in an Impressionist style. She worked as a copyist and restorer for Lord Halifax at his house at Temple Newsam, Leeds – a post probably organised by her father. His political connections also paved the way for her commission to paint *A Scene on the Terrace of the House of Commons*; a photograph by Sir John Benjamin Stone (1838–1914) in the National Portrait Gallery's collection, taken on 4 November 1909, records her with the painting *in situ*. Twenty years on from her youthful self-portrait she has succumbed to a formalised photographic representation of her supposedly 'at work', posing with her palette whilst wearing a large plumed Edwardian hat.

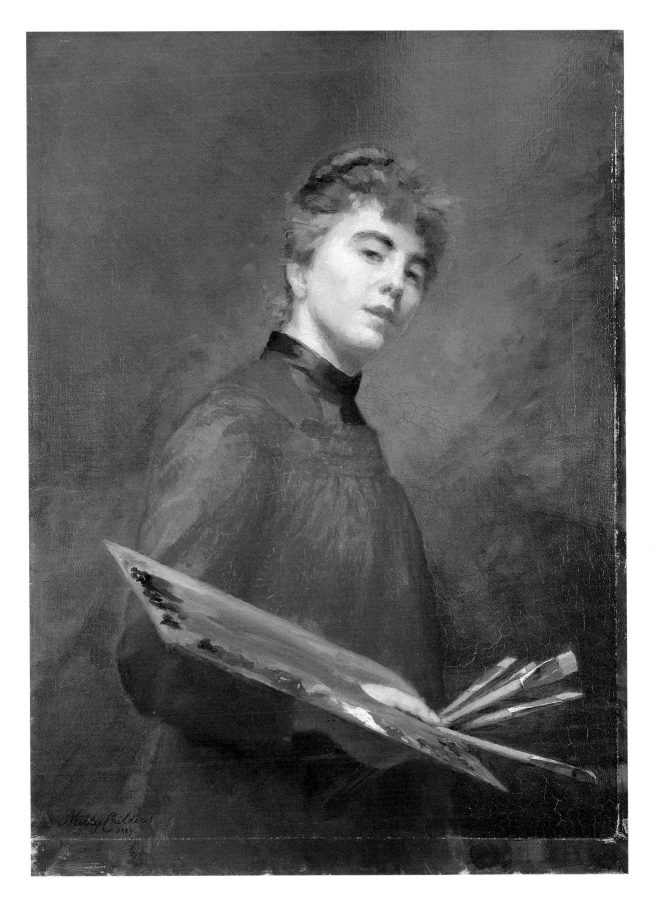

Lallie Charles (1869–1919) and Rita Martin (1875–1958)
with their sister Beaulah 'Bea' Martin
Published 1899
Toned carbon print from a whole-plate glass negative, 208 x 392mm (8¼ x 14⅜")
National Portrait Gallery, London (NPG x68948)

This photograph, assumed to have been taken by Lallie Charles (seen far right) is set in her studio 'The Nook' at 1 Titchfield Road, Regent's Park, London. It was certainly art-directed by Lallie. As her sister Rita (centre) was also a photographer we can assume that her image, too, is a self-conscious one, to be regarded as a type of self-portrait – and viewed in the same way as we view the mother-and-daughter image of Eveleen Myers (see p.51). Rita opened her own studio at 74 Baker Street in 1906 and the two sisters became the most commercially successful women portrait photographers of the first decade of the twentieth century.

The work is bursting with Victorian decorative detail. Varying patterns jostle with each other; a Chinese screen, vase and tea-set rub shoulders with oriental props and rugs, giving the studio a haphazard, bohemian air which contrasts with the corseted sisters who pose proudly amongst the two palms. Lallie (aided by her sisters) worked as a professional from 1897, and moved in 1907 from The Nook to 39a Curzon Street, Mayfair, where she became the foremost female portrait photographer of her day. The later studio was luxurious: Madame Yevonde, her assistant, reminisced 'The curtains were of rose-coloured silk, the chairs were upholstered in pink velvet and thick-piled carpet covered the floor.' Yevonde, who went on to become a noted photographer herself (see pp.78–9), was later to echo Lallie Charles's view that women made better photographers than men; Charles's feelings on this had been published in an article for *Every Woman's Encyclopaedia* (1912). Lallie's speciality was the 'pouter pigeon' look, in which her late Edwardian sitters were portrayed as beautiful, elegant and seemingly innocent, forever girlish, passive and pink.

Lallie married twice, her first husband introducing specific 'packaging' for her photographs – they were printed on pale-pink-toned papers, mounted in ivory-white folders embellished with grey lettering. Lallie Charles Martin, the sisters' niece, presented their surviving prints and negatives to the National Portrait Gallery in 1994.

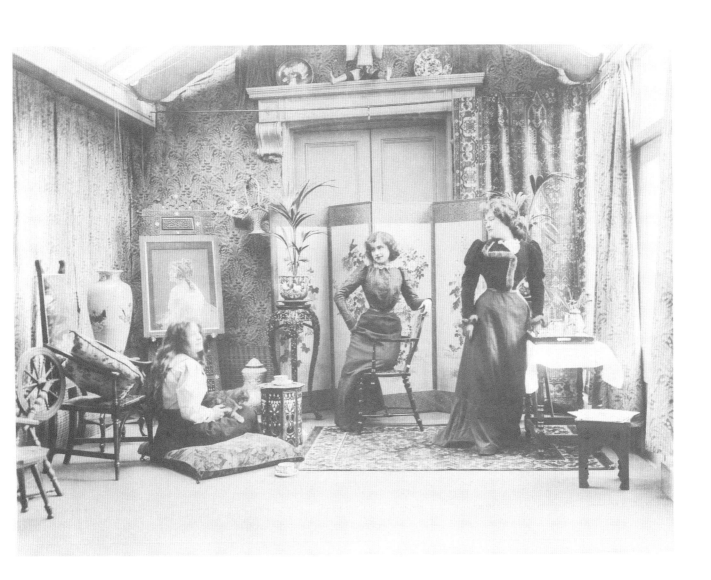

Gwen John (1876–1939)
*c.*1900
Oil on canvas, 610 x 378mm (24 x 14⅞")
National Portrait Gallery, London (NPG 4439)

Gwen John and her brother Augustus (1878–1961) grew up in Tenby, Wales, and trained together at the Slade School of Fine Art from 1895 to 1898. Gwen left the Slade, having won a prize for figure composition, and studied briefly at James Abbott McNeill Whistler's Académie Carmen in Paris from 1898 to 1899. Whistler (1834–1903) admired her sense of tone; her brother said that she was the 'greatest woman artist of her age' and that 'Fifty years after my death I shall be remembered as Gwen John's brother.' (Quoted in M. Holroyd, *Augustus John: The New Biography*, 1996.)

Gwen returned to London in 1900, when she exhibited with the New English Art Club, and later showed with her brother at Carfax and Co. Galleries. In 1904 she moved to France permanently and became involved with the sculptor Auguste Rodin, to whom she wrote 2,000 love letters and who introduced her to the leading figures of the avant-garde. In 1911 she moved to Meudon, a Paris suburb, and from then on lived and worked alone.

The American collector John Quinn was her only patron. He eventually owned at least eighteen of her paintings and fifty drawings and he included her painting *Girl Reading at the Window* (1911; now in the Museum of Modern Art, New York) in the Armory Show, America's first 'modern art' exhibition, in New York in 1913. That same year Gwen became a Catholic and painted works for the Convent of the Sisters of Charity at Meudon, including portraits of the nuns. She remained in France during World War I, spending most of the summers of 1915 to 1922 in Brittany. In 1922 she exhibited at the Salon d'Automne in Paris and in the *Modern English Artists* show at the Sculptors' Gallery, New York. Her only solo exhibition during her life was at the New Chenil Galleries in London in 1926. During the 1930s she painted less, living an increasingly solitary life, and died in Dieppe on 1 September 1939.

This self-assured self-portrait shows the 24-year-old artist in a confident, confrontational pose, hand on hip, looking straight out at us and boldly filling the entire space of the canvas. Colours and tonal values are subtle, oil paint gently dabbed onto the canvas with delicate obsessive precision, carefully rendering the folds and pleats of the bow around her neck and her russet blouse. The shape of her splayed hand echoes the 'puff' of the form of her gigot sleeve and brings to mind 'old master' self-portraits. There exists a similar though slightly later half-length self-portrait in the collection of the Tate; of the two this seems more imperious, but in both Gwen John suggests a very distinctive and refined personal quality of her own.

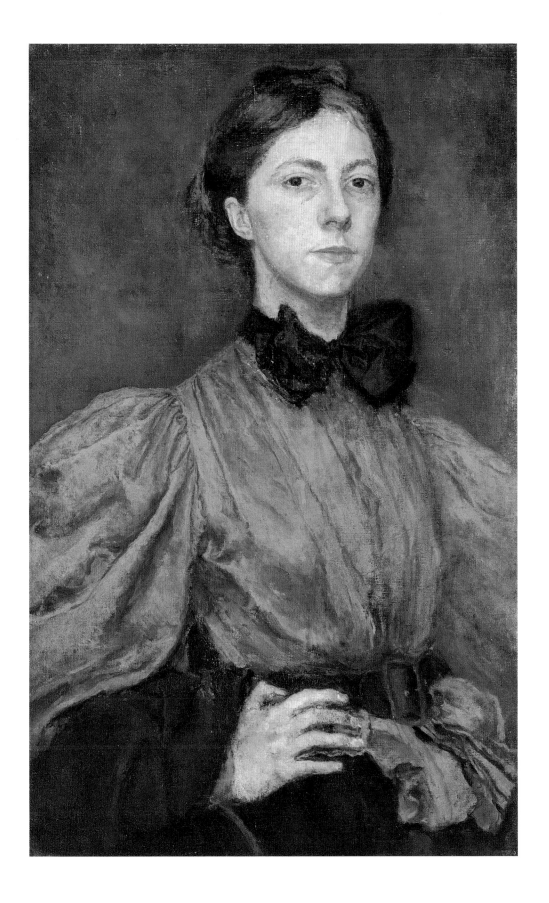

Eveleen Myers (1856–1937) and her daughter Silvia Constance Myers (1883–1957)
*c.*1900
Sepia platinotype, 247 x 192mm (9¾ x 7½")
National Portrait Gallery, London (NPG x68522)

Like many photographic self-portraits, for example Helen Chadwick's (see p.101), this image was self-evidently staged and it is clear that Eveleen Myers organised the pose and setting in addition to the inclusion of her only daughter in the portrait. It may be that it was a specific occasion she wished to record, as this is one of several images and Eveleen's gown is clearly very special. Deenagh Goold-Adams, Eveleen's granddaughter, wrote the following about her grandmother in her later life:

> she concocted her own hats much as a bird builds a nest but with considerable artistry
> … She never threw anything away and revived ancient confections by the famous
> 'Lucille' by sewing on new furbelows … She had something which is described in the
> jargon of today as 'star quality' and I am sure she would have been noticed in any age
> and in any walk of life.
> (Typescript with Myers papers, Trinity College, Cambridge)

Eveleen Myers, née Tennant, was the youngest of three sisters, born in Russell Square, London. Following her marriage in 1880 to the writer Frederic Myers (1834–1901), she moved to Leckhampton House, Cambridge, which had been especially designed for the couple by the architect William Marshall. As a young girl she was actively involved in the salon society of her family, and her mother introduced her to artists, writers and political figures. Both she and her sister Dorothy were painted by Sir John Everett Millais and George Frederic Watts (1817–1904) in works that were exhibited at the Royal Academy. Eveleen visited the Isle of Wight as a child and sat to the photographer Julia Margaret Cameron (1815–79). This occasion obviously made an impression as in 1888, ostensibly in order to record the childhood of her sons Leopold and Harold, she took up photography. She also owned original prints by Cameron. It is possible that she wished to make a portrait together with her elder child and only daughter to complement the series of her younger children. It is a perfectly poignant moment in time, utterly nostalgic and autobiographical: a mother and daughter.

Myers showed her work at the Linked Ring Salon in the 1890s and four of her works were illustrated in photogravure in the 1891 issue of *Sun Artists*. But after her husband died in 1901, Myers left their Cambridge home with her darkroom and studio and gave up photography. In 1991 the National Portrait Gallery acquired two of her personal albums, thereby enhancing an earlier collection of portraits which includes those of Robert Browning and W.E. Gladstone. Myers' work was featured, along with that of Olive Edis, in an exhibition at the Gallery entitled *Edwardian Women Photographers* in 1994.

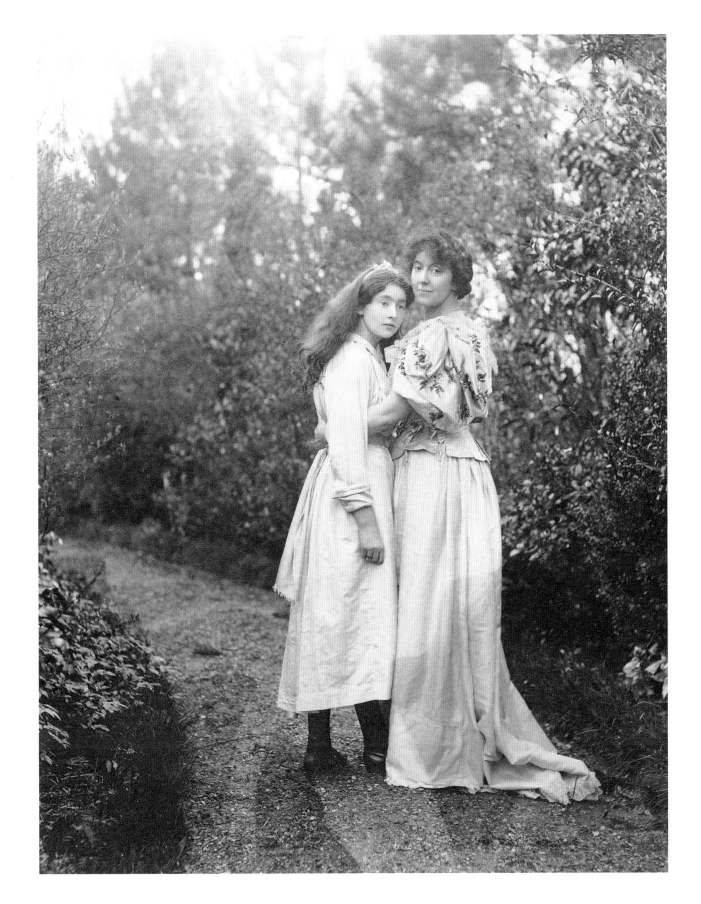

Bess Norriss (1878–1939)
*c.*1900–10
Watercolour, 238 x 187mm (9⅜ x 7⅜")
National Portrait Gallery, London (NPG 4054)

Born in Melbourne, Australia, where her father was a scientific chemist, Bess Norriss studied at Melbourne Art Gallery School and at the Slade School of Fine Art in London in 1905, specialising in watercolours and miniatures. In 1908 she married J. Nevin Tait, the UK representative of and partner in the Australian theatrical company J. & N. Tait. They had one son and one daughter and lived in Church Street, Chelsea.

Bess belonged to the Society of Women Artists and exhibited at the Royal Academy of Arts and the Paris Salon (1908–36), the Goupil Gallery and the Grosvenor Gallery, both in London. She also exhibited in America and in Australia when she returned home on trips. She often portrayed musicians in her miniatures, but she also worked on a larger scale in watercolour. A member of the Royal Society for Painting in Watercolour, and from 1907 the Royal Society of Miniature Painters, her paintings were reproduced in the *Studio* and the *Connoisseur* magazines. In *Who's Who in Art* (1934) her recreations are listed as theatre, reading and music, and her club as the 'Soroptimist'. Francis Derwent Wood (1871–1926) made a bronze bust of her in 1921–2, which was purchased by the Chantrey Bequest for the Tate (then the National Gallery, Millbank) in 1926.

Portraying herself here with a jaunty hat and a smile, she gives the impression of a positive frame of mind. The fact that this is a quick sketch enhances the feeling of something dashed off for fun, not a full-blown, serious attempt at a portrait, but this too could be interpreted as part of her character and linked to her choice of medium – watercolour being essentially one of quick marks and decisions.

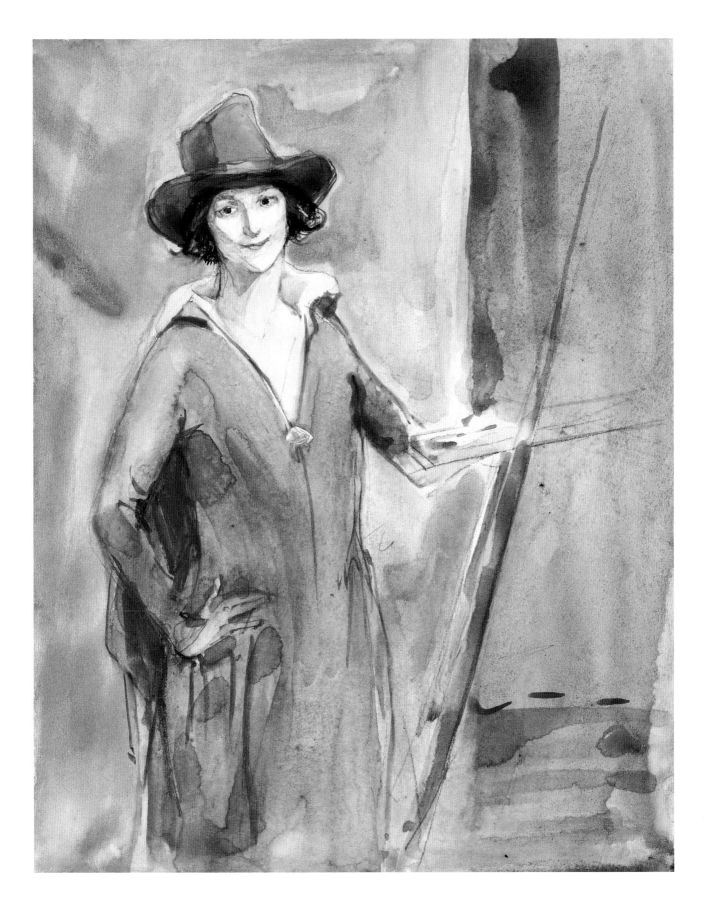

Sylvia Pankhurst (1882–1960)
*c.*1906
Chalk, 663 x 511mm (26⅛ x 20⅛")
National Portrait Gallery, London (NPG 4999)

Born in Manchester, the second of the suffragette Emmeline Pankhurst's (1858–1928) three daughters, Sylvia Pankhurst won a scholarship to the Manchester Municipal School of Art. Here she won several prizes, including the Procter Memorial Travelling Scholarship, which enabled her to visit Florence and Venice in 1902 specifically to view mosaics. In the spring of 1903 she returned home to execute a commission (organised by her mother) for murals for Pankhurst Hall, Salford, which had been built by the Independent Labour Party to honour her father, Richard Marsden Pankhurst (1835–98). Later that year Sylvia came first in a national competition for a scholarship to the Royal College of Art and so moved to London.

In 1904 she joined in her first political demonstration, at the Albert Hall, and spent her Christmas holidays back home in Manchester painting banners which read 'Votes for Women', in readiness for the General Election of 1906. Whilst studying she continued to be active in London's East End branch of the Women's Social and Political Union, a suffrage organisation that had been jointly founded by her mother and elder sister Christabel (1880–1958). She designed the members' card for the organisation and in 1906 was imprisoned for the first time for her part in a WSPU protest. This drawing can possibly be dated from that time, as she appears to be wearing prison clothing. It is also known that on her release Sylvia gave the press sketches she had made 'inside' in order to expose the dire conditions. She was later imprisoned many times and went on hunger strikes. In 1913 she left the WSPU and the following year her objections to World War I stood in sharp contrast to the supporting views of Emmeline and Christabel. Her publications include *The Suffragette* (1911), *Writ on a Cold Slate*, a collection of poems (1922), *The Suffragette Movement: An Intimate Account of Persons and Ideas* (1931), *The Home Front* (1932), *The Life of Emmeline Pankhurst: The Suffragette Struggle for Women's Citizenship* and *Myself When Young* (1938). Her campaign for independence for Ethiopia was championed in her book *Ethiopia: A Cultural History* (1955). Sylvia's art was subsumed by her political life (see pp.20–21) but in 1908 she did produce a set of paintings that were reproduced in the *London Magazine* under the heading *Women Workers of England*, depicting shoemakers, Scottish fishwives, cotton workers and 'pit-brow lasses'.

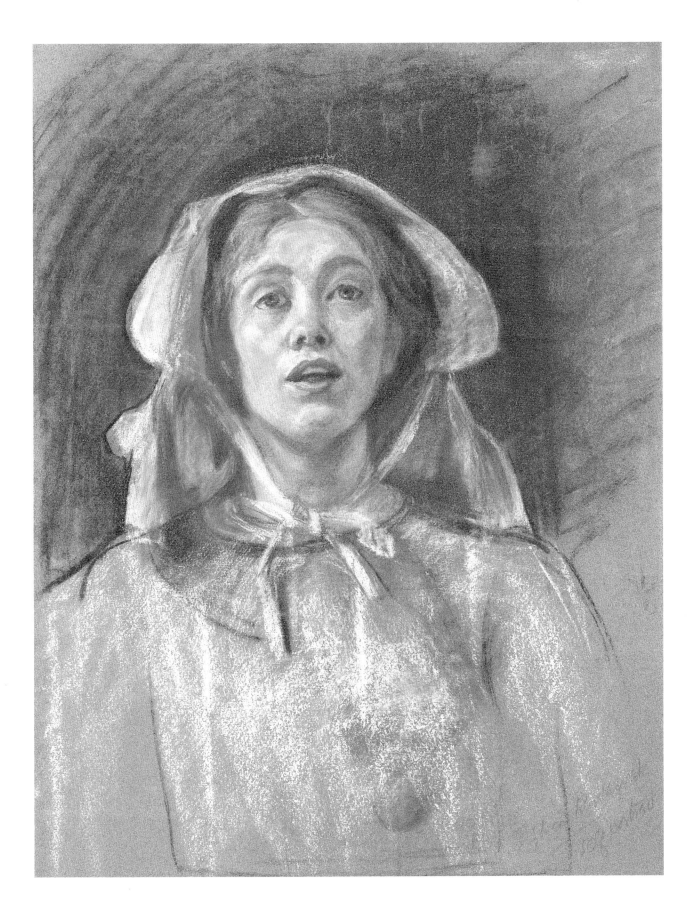

Dame Laura Knight (1877–1970)
1913
Oil on canvas, 1524 x 1276mm (60 x 50¼")
National Portrait Gallery, London (NPG 4839)

At the age of fifty-nine, in 1936, Dame Laura Knight was the first woman to be created Royal Academician since Angelica Kauffmann and Mary Moser in the eighteenth century. This fact reveals her popular success as an artist in her own lifetime, and also perhaps her singular ambition. Born in Long Eaton, Derbyshire, she studied at Nottingham School of Art, where she met and married fellow student Harold Knight in 1903. They went to live in Staithes on the Yorkshire coast in 1894, and between 1908 and 1919 were members of the artists' colony in Newlyn, Cornwall. This portrait was painted there, the model Laura's friend and fellow artist Ella Naper (1886–1972).

Knight comments on the role of the woman artist by a bravura display of painting techniques, a complicated composition, and the pointed inclusion of a naked female model, traditionally painted by men. The painting is powerful and physically imposing, the scale life-size, and the whole is underpinned with flamboyant colour. The model's malleable pink flesh is lurid against the orange backdrop. Knight's red cardigan was a favourite (she had bought it at a jumble sale in Penzance for half a crown); it appears in a number of other paintings and here it vibrates with spots of colour painted in a thick impasto style and is the first focus of our attention when we confront the painting. Three back views are counterposed in a triangular composition, a visual tactic that underlines the relationship between artist and model, model and canvas, canvas and artist: we follow Knight's gaze and profile towards the female model and then across to the painted form emerging on her canvas. Knight's black hat is stark against the unpainted part of the canvas and her profile is clearly delineated, anchoring the work – an integral part of a highly organised composition. She manages to arrest our attention despite showing us her back, an unusual stance for a self-view.

Knight was an official war artist from 1940 to 1945 and in 1946 was commissioned to make a pictorial record of the Nuremberg Trials. Renowned for making an old Rolls-Royce her miniature travelling studio, she was also famous for her *plein-air* paintings of gypsies, circus performers and studies of the Diaghilev Ballet. In 1965 she had a retrospective exhibition of her work in the Diploma Gallery at the Royal Academy, the first woman to be so honoured. Her work is in many public collections including the Imperial War Museum, the National Portrait Gallery and the Tate.

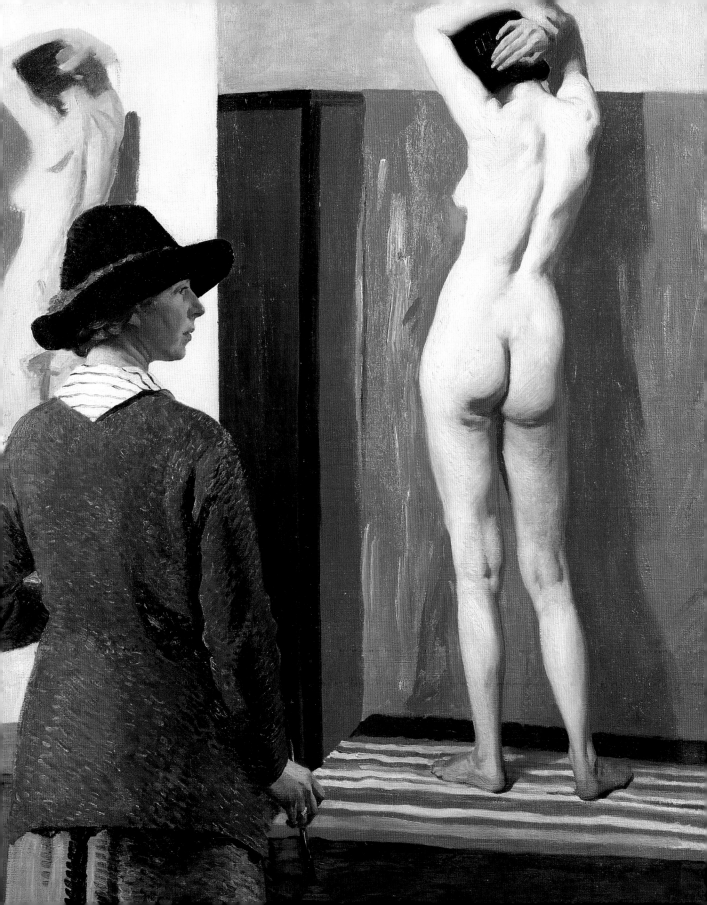

Olive Edis (1876–1955)
1918
Sepia platinotype, 133 x 79mm (5½ x 3⅛")
National Portrait Gallery, London (NPG x7960)

Olive Edis grew up in Wimpole Street, London, where her father was a gynaecologist. By the early 1900s she had established herself as a portrait photographer. In 1903 she went into partnership with her sister Katharine (1880–1963), opening a studio in Sheringham, a seaside resort in Norfolk. The sisters specialised in both studio and 'at home' portraits, also photographing local fishermen and celebrities. This partnership was dissolved when Katharine married but Olive kept her Sheringham studio throughout her life. From 1913 to 1933 her professional London address was at 34 Colville Terrace, W11, where she lived with her mother and, after 1928, with her husband Edwin Galsworthy (1861-1947). From 1912 she made autochrome colour photographs of people and flowers, and in 1913 she was one of eight people elected to become a member of the Royal Photographic Society, winning a bronze medal for a portrait which, said the *British Journal of Photography,* 'was almost equalled, we think, by her "Sweet Peas". As portrait studies either of these will take a good deal of beating, the colour and gradation being almost perfect and extremely delicate in both of them.' In 1914 she became a fellow of the RPS and patented her autochrome viewer – one of which she left in her will, with a selection of her work, to the National Portrait Gallery.

By the end of World War I Edis was an established colour photographer. This portrait dates from 1918 when she was commissioned by the Government to record the work of the British Women's Services in France and Flanders during the war. Her start was delayed until March 1919, by which time the conflict was over, but nevertheless she covered 2,000 miles in a month of demanding work. She shows herself bending slightly forward over one of the three cameras she took with her on the trip. Her five-string pearl necklace is the same one that she wore in an earlier self-portrait (1912) in the guise of Fortitude. Between July and November 1920 she went to photograph the Rockies. This was a commission from the Canadian Pacific Railway, and she used their specially equipped photographic railway carriage to carry out her work. 'Miss Edis has been very successful in her reproduction of Indian types [Native American Indians], their full dress regalia are admirably shown.' (*Financier,* 9 May 1921.) Sadly none of this work has survived.

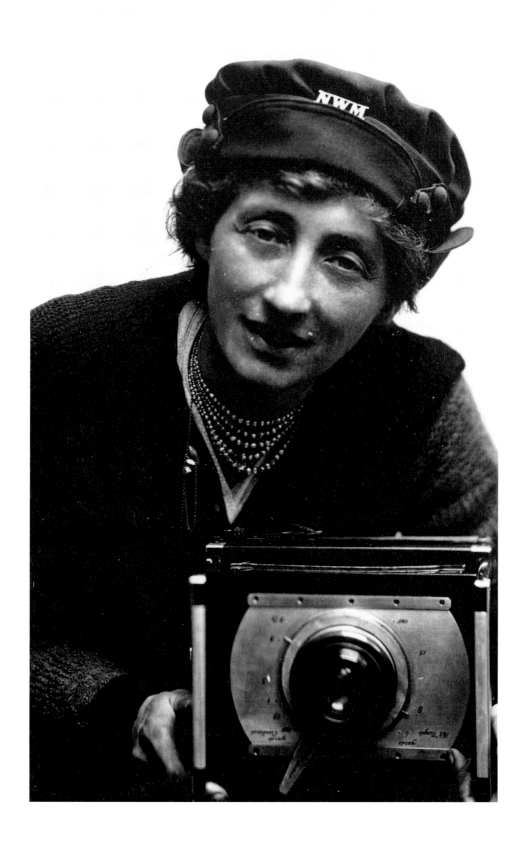

Dame Ethel Walker (1861–1951)
*c.*1925
Oil on canvas, 613 x 508mm (24⅛ x 20")
National Portrait Gallery, London (NPG 5301)

Dame Ethel Walker was born in Edinburgh. She attended Putney School of Art, Westminster School of Art and the Slade School of Fine Art during different periods between 1883 and 1922. Velázquez (1599–1660), the Impressionists and Walter Sickert (1872–98), whose evening classes she attended, were her main influences. She exhibited at the Royal Academy from 1898 onwards and joined the New English Art Club in 1900. Her first one-person show was at the Redfern Gallery, Cork Street, London, in 1927. She had a studio by the Thames in Chelsea (she was known as a 'Cheyne Walker' – one of a group of women artists who had trained at the Slade, belonged to the New English Art Club and lived in Cheyne Walk). She also had a cottage in Robin Hood's Bay, Yorkshire, where she spent time with her wire-haired fox terriers and painted seascapes outdoors. She represented Britain in the Venice Biennale in 1930 and 1932, and her painting *Nausicaa* (now in the Tate's collection) represented British art at the 1939 World Trade Fair in Chicago.

This portrait has real presence and a feeling of spontaneity, echoing the work of the French painter and printmaker Berthe Morisot (1841–95) in its impasto and textured brushwork. There is a slightly raffish quality to the masculine tie worn askew, whilst the decorative collar of her yellow jacket is visually arresting. Walker's portraits, still lifes and landscape paintings show a sensibility which is more convincing than in her larger visionary compositions. Walker was said to have been an eccentric character with a terse wit, confidence in her own abilities and a 'furious energy'.

Elected honorary president of the Women's International Art Club in 1932, she was made an Associate Member of the Royal Academy in 1940 and a Dame Commander of the British Empire in 1943. The Tate held a retrospective exhibition of her work (together with that of Gwen John and Frances Hodgkins) in 1951. Her work is held in numerous public collections including the Royal Collection, the Courtauld Institute of Art, the Musée d'Art Moderne de la Ville de Paris, and at York City Art Gallery and Leeds City Art Gallery.

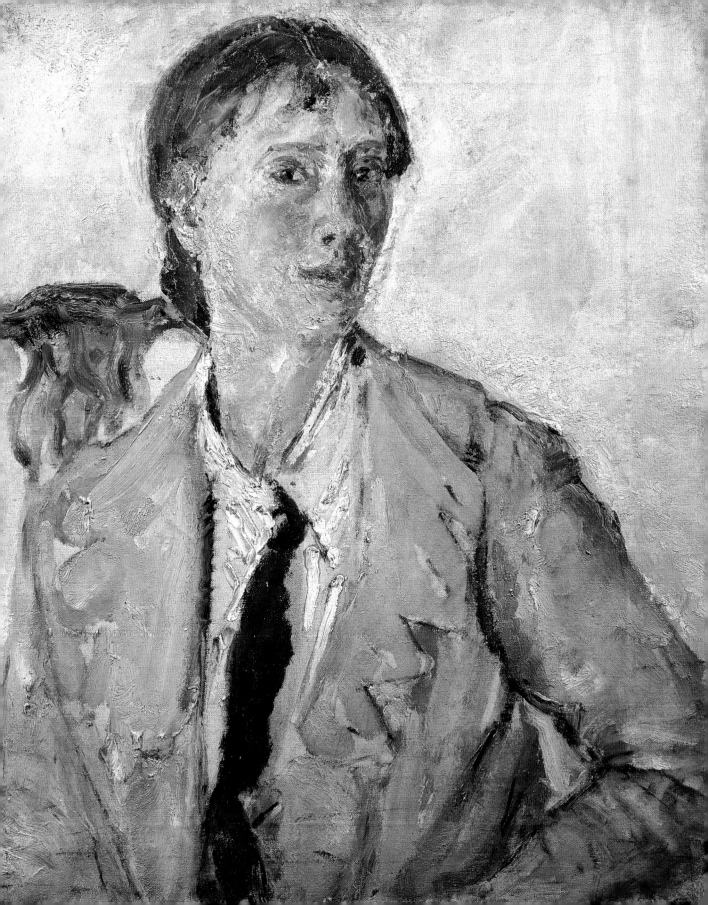

Eileen Agar (1899–1991)
1927
Oil on canvas, 765 x 641mm (30⅛ x 25¼")
National Portrait Gallery, London (NPG 5881)

Eileen Agar moved to England from her birthplace, Buenos Aires, Argentina, in 1906. She studied at the Byam Shaw School of Art (1919–20), at the Leon Underwood School of Painting and Sculpture (1920–21), where her peers included Henry Moore (1898–1986) and Gertrude Hermes (see pp.86–7), and then at the Slade School of Fine Art (1922–6). The death of her father in 1925 provided her with a private income which enabled 'une vie d'artiste' in Paris between 1928 and 1930. In the late 1930s Agar found herself in the milieu of the Surrealist avant-garde. She was the only British woman painter included in the International Surrealist Exhibition held at the New Burlington Galleries, London, in 1936. Paul Nash (1889–1946) and Sir Herbert Read (1893–1968) selected her for inclusion in the show and described themselves as 'enchanted by the rare quality of her talent, the product of a highly sensitive imagination and a feminine clairvoyance'. (Quoted in D. Ades, 'Notes on two women Surrealist painters: Eileen Agar and Ithell Colquhoun', *Oxford Art Journal*, iii/I, 1980, p.37.) She spent the summer of 1937 at Mougins with Nash (with whom she also had an affair between 1935 and 1940), Paul Éluard (1895–1952), Sir Roland Penrose (1900–84), Man Ray (1890–1976) and Pablo Picasso (1881–1973). World War II disrupted her painting and she did not start working again seriously until 1946. She exhibited with the Surrealists in New York, Tokyo, Paris and Amsterdam.

Painted onto coarse canvas, this work bears the confidence of youth. Agar portrays herself in a robust three-quarter pose using black to delineate her features. The green that she wears recurs in the shadows on her face and her auburn hair is rendered in impasto. The work is painted in a loose post-Impressionist style.

Eileen Agar's work is in the collections of the Tate, the Scottish National Gallery of Modern Art and Leeds City Art Gallery. Birch and Conran Fine Art, London, gave her a retrospective in 1987, which revived her career. Agar wrote her autobiography *A Look at My Life* with Andrew Lambirth in 1988. This painting was purchased from the artist's niece in 1986.

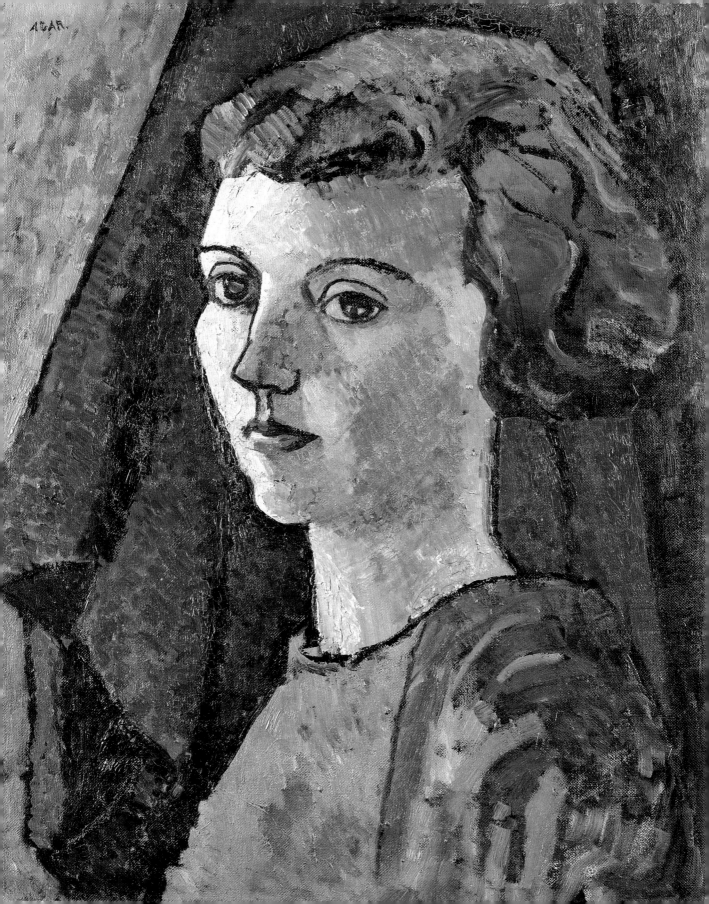

Paule Vézelay (1892–1984)
*Harmony, c.*1927–9
Oil on canvas, 651 x 543mm (25⅝ x 21⅜")
National Portrait Gallery, London (NPG 6003)

From art school in Bristol, the city where she was born, Marjorie Watson-Williams went on to study at the Slade School of Fine Art in 1911. Her first one-person show was in Brussels in 1920 and it was from there that she first visited Paris. 'English art then bored me to tears,' she said. In 1926 she made her first abstract drawing, changed her name to Paule Vézelay (inspired by the medieval Burgundian basilica village) and settled in Paris.

Entitled *Harmony*, this self-portrait reflects the abstract style of Vézelay's work. The muted colours – pale grey, pink and mauve – enhance the dreamy quality. Stylistically it is reminiscent of work by Russian Rayonnists or Italian Futurists.

Vézelay joined the Société Abstraction-Création in 1934, becoming friends with Jean Arp (1887–1966) and his wife Sophie Taeuber-Arp (1889–1943), and in 1938 she exhibited in Milan with Arp, Wassily Kandinsky (1866–1944) and Kurt Seligmann (1900–62). In September 1939 the onset of war forced her return to Bristol, where she made abstract ink studies of bomb damage, took remarkable photographs, and made pastel drawings of barrage balloons (now in the collection of the Imperial War Museum, London). On her return to Paris in 1946 Vézelay found that she had lost all the paintings and possessions she had left in France. Back in London in the 1950s she produced textile designs for Heal's. The Grosvenor Gallery held a retrospective of her work in 1968 and she featured in the BBC 2 programme *Women of Our Century* in August 1984. In 1982 Vézelay declined to represent her work in the *Women's Art Show 1550–1970*, held at the Nottingham Castle Museum, arguing that her position was primarily that of an artist rather than a woman artist.

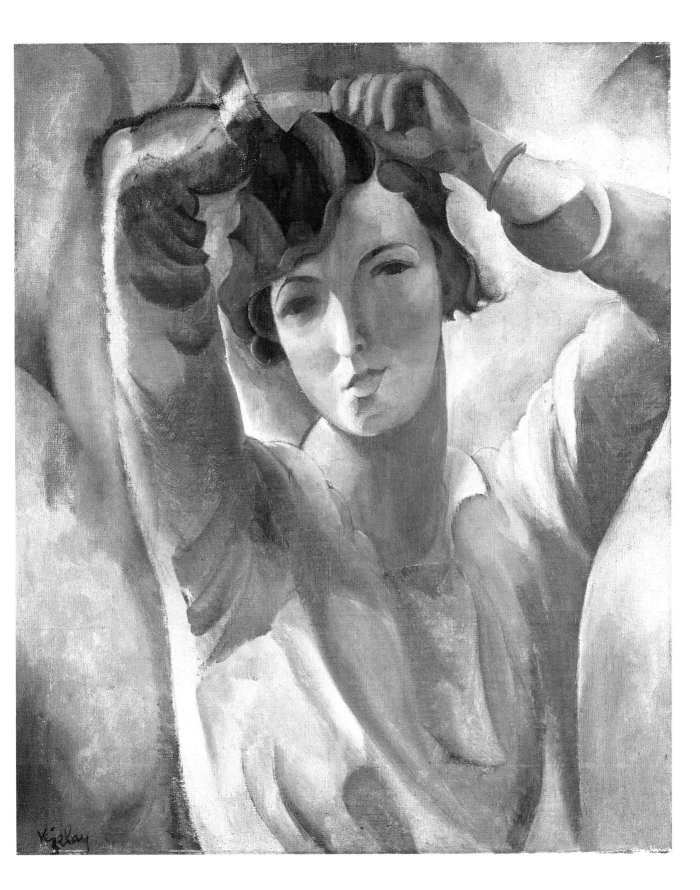

Doris Zinkeisen (1898–1991)
Exhibited 1929
Oil on canvas, 1072 x 866mm (42¼ x 34⅛")
National Portrait Gallery, London (NPG 6487)

Doris Zinkeisen was born in Gareloch, Argyllshire, but her father's family were originally from Bohemia and had settled in Scotland two hundred years before. Like her younger sister, Anna, Doris attended Harrow School of Art and won a scholarship to the Royal Academy. She was awarded Bronze, Silver and Gold medals at the Salon in Paris. On leaving the Academy she went to work in stage design for the actor-manager Sir Nigel Playfair (1874–1934), who also wanted her to sing, but she was adamant that she should remain 'behind the scenes'. She designed costumes and sets for the Old Vic Theatre productions of *Arms and the Man* and *Richard III* with Sir Ralph Richardson, Dame Sybil Thorndike and Laurence Olivier, Baron Olivier (also creating Olivier's make-up for the film). She painted the mural for the Verandah Grill on the *Queen Mary* in 1936 and in 1938 she wrote *Designing for the Stage*. During World War II she was commissioned by the War Artists Advisory Committee and was one of the first artists to enter Belsen in April 1945, where she stayed for three days. Two of the paintings she made there can be seen in the Imperial War Museum, London.

Like her sister (see p.85), Doris wears a good deal of make-up in her self-portrait and uses dramatic colouring to enhance the effect. The rather exotic, heavily embroidered Chinese shawl draped off her shoulders lends a provocative air. She seems about to leave the set, pulling aside the black curtain with a hand half-covered by the black edging of the shawl, its manicured fingernails painted an eye-catching red. The portrait was painted mostly in her hotel bedroom in Sydney, Australia, whilst she was on a world tour. It was exhibited at the Royal Academy in 1929 under her married name, Mrs Grahame Johnstone, both ironically denying her connection with the creation of the image and asserting her social position.

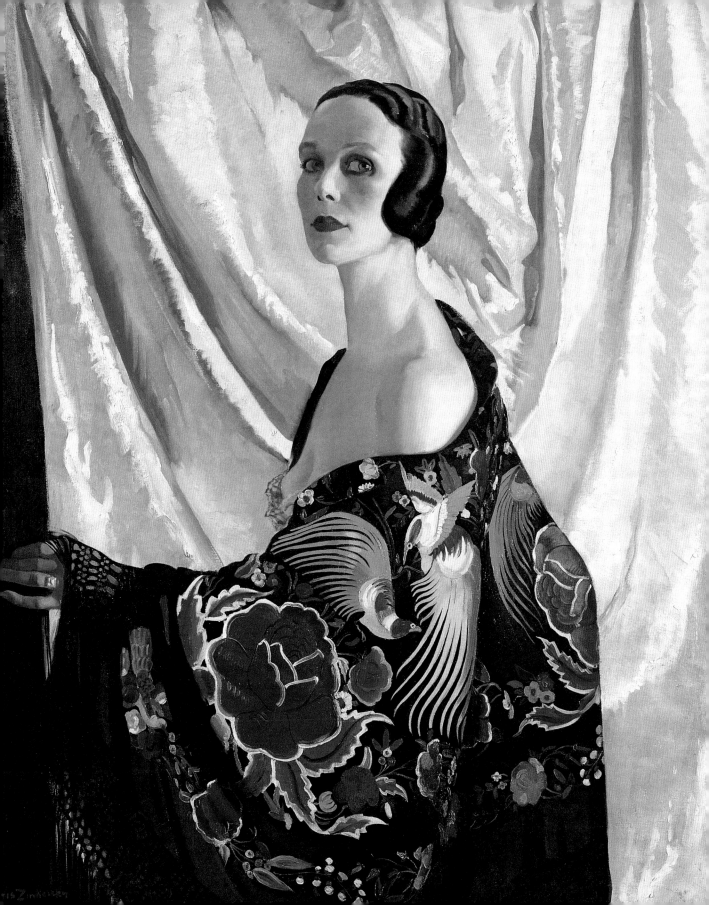

Jessica Dismorr (1885–1939)
*c.*1929
Oil on gesso board, 609 x 484mm (24 x 19")
National Portrait Gallery, London (NPG 6393)

Born in Gravesend, Kent, Jessica Dismorr studied at the Atelier de la Palette, Paris, with Jacques-Emile Blanche (1861–1942) and John Duncan Fergusson (1874–1961) from 1910 to 1913, and during that time was closely associated with the British Fauves in Paris. On her return to London in 1913 she met Percy Wyndham Lewis (1882–1957), and for twelve years they were both committed to writing and making images. In June 1914 Dismorr signed the Vorticist manifesto in his magazine *Blast* and in 1915 she exhibited with the Vorticists at the Doré Galleries, London, contributing to *Blast 2*. In 1916 she showed with the Allied Artists Association and the American collector John Quinn bought her work to exhibit with that of other Vorticists in New York. Throughout this period she also published poetry, and this became a substitute for her painting during World War I, when she nursed the wounded in France.

In 1920 she was part of the sole exhibition of Wyndham Lewis's ten-artist-strong Group X, and in 1925 had her first one-person show at the Mayor Gallery, London. This was also the year that she came into her inheritance, which gave her less money than she had anticipated and more in the way of problems, as fellow artists resented her financial independence. She was elected to the Seven and Five Society in 1926, which was at the time the most progressive exhibiting society in London and this kept her involved with the 'new' avant-garde: Henry Moore, Ben Nicholson (1894–1982) and Barbara Hepworth (see pp.88–9) were part of the group.

Yettie Frankfort, a friend of Dismorr, said of her, 'as we became acquainted she reminded me of a dormant volcano, snowy and fiery ... inner conflict or rather a precarious balance of conflicting tendencies was of her essence'. Dismorr suffered from depression throughout her life and had more than one breakdown. Another friend, Fay Asher, spoke about 'her withdrawn quality' and said that 'self-destruction was inevitable'. Dismorr hanged herself aged fifty-four at home in Hampstead, London.

This painting has an almost tentative quality; it seems hardly to exist, the whites of the prepared gesso board emanating translucence and fragility, the pale colours brushed on so lightly. There is a sketchiness that belies the solidity of the figure looming towards us within the space of the room and of the robust kitchen chair she sits on. The rough calligraphic marks indicate the paintings behind her but of course are merely ciphers for the real thing. Dismorr's work is in the collections of the Tate and the Victoria and Albert Museum.

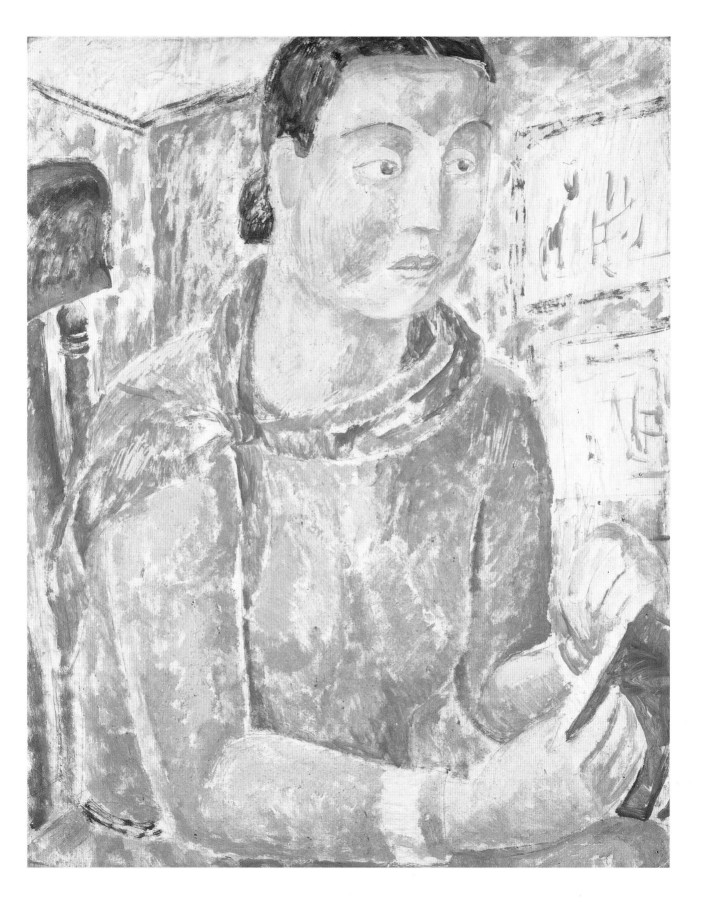

Ithell Colquhoun (1906–88)
1930s?
Ink and wash, 458 x 324mm (18 x 12¾")
National Portrait Gallery, London (NPG 6486)

Poet, author and painter, student of the occult, of alchemy, Celtic lore and mythology, Ithell Colquhoun was born in Assam, India. She studied under Henry Tonks (1862–1937) at the Slade School of Fine Art from 1927 to 1931 and won the Slade Summer Competition Prize in 1929. After this she went to Paris where she met Man Ray, René Magritte (1898–1967), Marcel Duchamp, Salvador Dalí (1904–89) and André Breton, who had published his first *Manifeste du Surréalisme* in 1924. She travelled further afield in Europe, and on her return in 1936 held her first one-person show in Cheltenham, the same year she showed with the Fine Art Society. That year the New Burlington Gallery held the first International Surrealist Exhibition and Colquhoun attended group meetings with artists such as Sir Roland Penrose, John Banting (1902–72) and Eileen Agar (see pp.62–3). In the 1940s she married Toni del Renzio (they later divorced), publisher of the Surrealist magazine *Arson*. Whilst living in Hampstead she wrote Surrealist poetry and started to experiment with 'automatic' painting processes; she also began visiting Cornwall regularly. In 1947 she showed at the Mayor Gallery, London, and in 1948 at the Leicester Galleries, London. In September 1949 she bought Gluck's Hampstead studio for £2,500. In 1950 Colquhoun moved to Paul, near Penzance, and showed in Berlin and Hamburg. The Newlyn Orion Gallery held a retrospective of her work in 1976 and the Tate bought her painting *Scylla* (1938) in 1977. Her writings include *The Living Stones* (1957), *Goose of Hermogenes* (1961) and *Sword of Wisdom* (1975).

Ithell Colquhoun's portrait of the archaeologist Humfry Payne is in the National Portrait Gallery's collection. The preparatory drawing for this has similarities to her self-portrait – there is a translucency suggested by the ink wash on tracing paper. In her own portrait she makes use of the element of chance, allowing the ink to swirl and flow on the surface of the paper. This 'semi-control' of the medium imparts a feeling of ambiguity and uncertainty – it is experimental, and in this way is an apt visual correlative of her character and her life as a spiritualist.

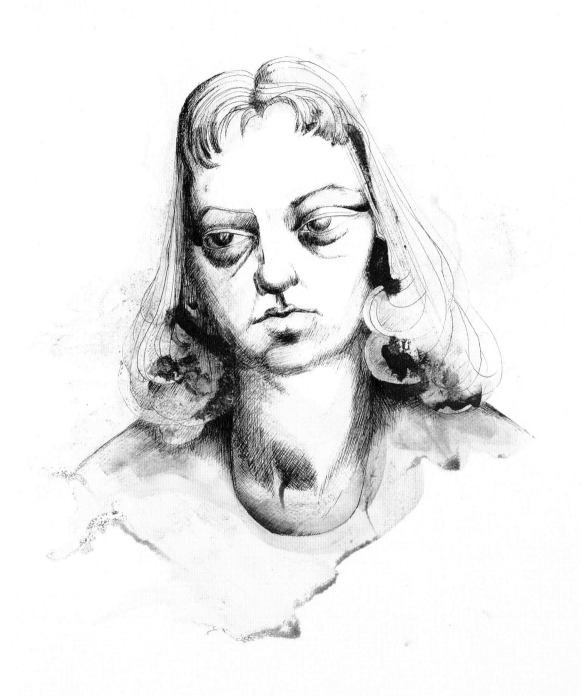

Dorothy Wilding (1893–1976)
1930s
Chlorobromide print, 207 x 148mm (8⅛ x 5⅞")
National Portrait Gallery, London (NPG x27403)

Dorothy Wilding was born in Gloucester, the youngest of nine children, and at the age of four she was sent to live with her childless aunt and uncle in Cheltenham. This early experience may well account for her determination to become financially independent and well known. Her ambition was to be an actress or a painter but aged sixteen she bought a camera and tripod and became a photographer.

Wilding moved to London in 1910, becoming an apprentice retoucher in a photographic studio and, having saved enough money, by the age of twenty-one she opened her first portrait studio. This was a success and she moved the business from George Square to Regent Street in 1918, expanding her mainly female staff to seven. Here she consolidated her style of using artificial light, and mounting her portraits first onto tissue, then onto tinted card and finally onto a larger card, which bore her specially designed logo on the reverse. She made a loveless marriage in 1920, divorcing in 1932, and that same year, aged thirty-nine, she married the interior decorator Thomas 'Rufus' Leighton Pearce, who transformed her new Bond Street studio with a clean modernist design. In 1933 she won third prize in the 13th Annual Competition of American Photography and received positive press reviews for her work.

In 1937 Wilding took the coronation portraits of George VI and his family (she was later to become the first woman photographer granted 'By Appointment' status to the royal family). At the end of the year she moved to New York to open a studio (it was run concurrent with the one in London until 1956 and had a staff of thirty-seven). She operated a huge stand camera by means of a cable release, directing assistants to move lights, attend sitters and arrange poses. This self-portrait gives a good idea of her extrovert, sunny personality. It records an exuberant pose with a flashing smile and indicates the physical scale of her camera. Wilding's clients included Tallulah Bankhead, Gladys Cooper, Yul Brynner, Harry Belafonte, the Zinkeisen sisters and the Duke and Duchess of Windsor. The trademark white studio blocks that she used as abstract counterpoints to her sitters' poses became highly fashionable. She again took the royal portraits on Coronation Day and studies from her 1952 portrait of Queen Elizabeth II were used for stamps and coinage. In 1958 her autobiography, *In Pursuit of Perfection*, was published, and she sold her business. The National Portrait Gallery holds over 900 of her original negatives and prints presented by her sister and studio manager Mrs Susan Morton in 1976.

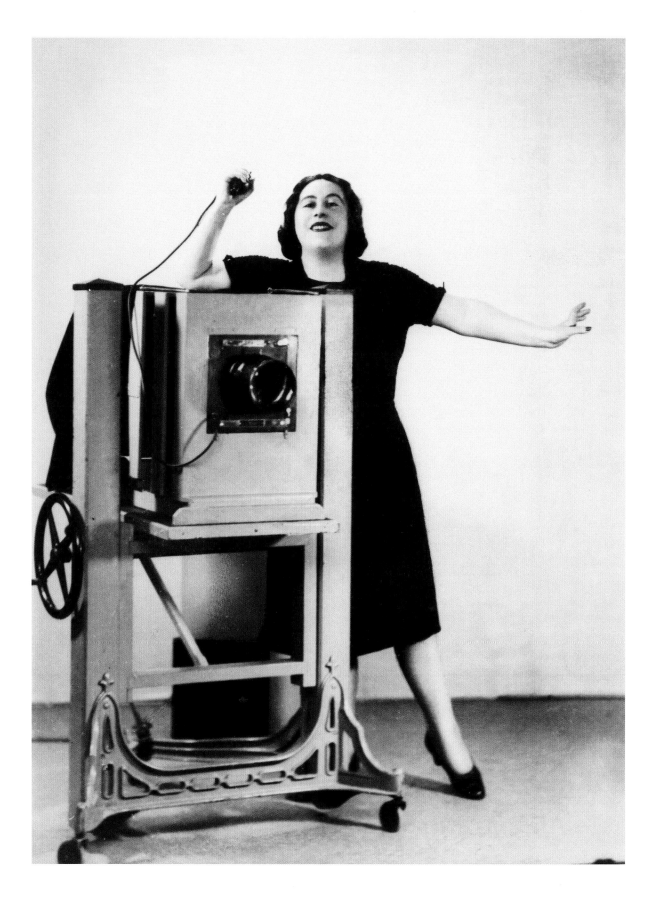

Susie Cooper (1902–95)
*c.*1933
Ceramic, 314 x 159mm (12⅜ x 6¼")
National Portrait Gallery, London (NPG 6375)

Susie Cooper was born in Burslem, Staffordshire, and worked in the Potteries for sixty-four years. She was the most influential and important woman in the British pottery industry of the twentieth century and in 1940 she became the only woman to be created Royal Designer for Industry. Her business motto was 'Elegance combined with utility'.

Cooper studied at the Burslem School of Art, joining Gray's Pottery, Hanley, in 1922. This led to her showing work at the British Empire Exhibition two years later. On her twenty-seventh birthday Cooper set up her own business, the Susie Cooper Pottery, and ran this in one form or another until 1980. Innovative in her approach to design and decoration, she was an exemplary employer who also knew how to take advantage of her skilled female workforce. This meant that certain decorative patterns were allocated to younger 'paintresses' and by 1933 she was employing more than forty women to reproduce her distinctive art-deco designs. During this period she also worked closely with the Universal Transfer Company, creating a type of multi-coloured lithographic printed decoration which was indistinguishable from hand-painting, a development that still benefits the pottery industry today. In 1950 she bought a porcelain factory and with the help of her husband, the architect Cecil Barker (whom she married in 1938), started to manufacture for the first time, but she continued to 'buy in' earthenware products to her design. Her work was shown at the Exposition Internationale, Paris, in 1937, and at the Festival of Britain in 1951.

Cooper designed the 'Cooper's Can' shaped container, a classic that was in constant production for around thirty years, and she immortalised the 'Swinging Sixties' with a design called 'Carnaby Daisy'. Her ability to react to the changing times and styles around her and her business acumen were integral to her success. She joined the Wedgwood Group in 1966, becoming a Director and Senior Designer for them until 1972. She was awarded an honorary doctorate by the Royal College of Art in 1987, and the Order of the British Empire in 1979. In 1987 the Victoria and Albert Museum and the City Museum and Art Gallery, Stoke-on-Trent, staged a retrospective of her work entitled *Susie Cooper Productions*.

Cooper's self-portrait is one of four similar designs made in the early 1930s. Initially it hung in her London showroom and subsequently in her studio. The lustre-painted curls hark back to the lustreware of Gray's Pottery, where she learnt her hand-painting technique. The pierrot-like mask, with the obviously painted red bow lips, is reminiscent of a fragile, innocent ceramic doll's head, an appearance which belies Cooper's independence and productivity.

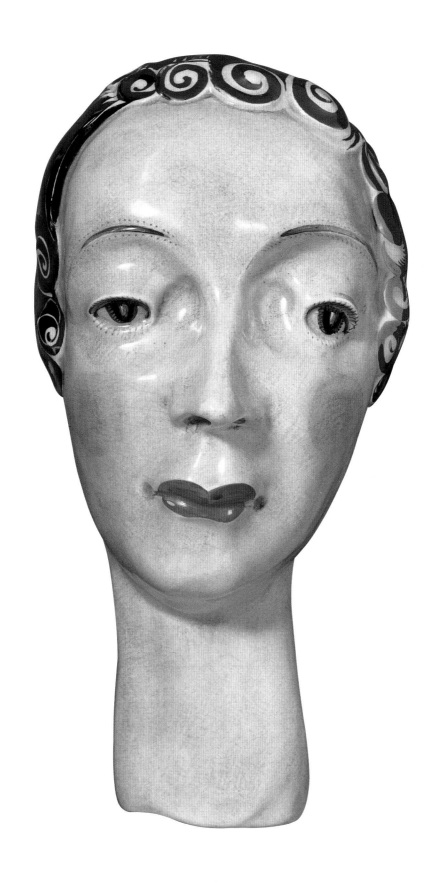

Lee Miller (1907–77)
1939
Modern bromide print from an original negative, 194 x 243mm (7⅝ x 9⅝")
National Portrait Gallery, London (NPG P873)

'Discovered' in 1927 by Condé Nast, Lee Miller became a model for American *Vogue* and posed for their staff photographer Edward Steichen (1879–1973) and for George Hoyningen-Huene (1900–68). However, she quickly became bored with being in front of the camera and she decided to move to Paris to learn the art of photography herself from Man Ray. In 1929 she became his student, collaborator, lover and muse, and it was at this time that by accident they discovered the process of solorisation, a particular method of combining a positive and negative image simultaneously. Man Ray produced his famous image of her floating lips, *Observatory Time – The Lovers* (1934), when she terminated their relationship to marry an Egyptian, Aziz Eloui, only later to begin an affair with the painter and writer Roland Penrose, who was to become her second husband. In January 1940 she became a staff photographer for *Vogue* in London, and was paid £8 per week. In 1941 she was appointed a US war correspondent, documenting the liberation of Paris and scenes from Dachau. (Doris Zinkeisen was also in Belsen painting as part of a commission by the War Artists Advisory Committee in April 1945; see p.66.)

Prior to marrying Penrose in 1947, Miller wrote to him announcing that she was pregnant. 'Let me know how you feel about being a parent – sure you want it? And why? There is only one thing – MY WORK ROOM IS NOT GOING TO BE A NURSERY. How about your studio? HA. HA.' (Quoted in A. Penrose, *The Lives of Lee Miller*, 1988, p.183.) She continued to take photographs, notably of the guests visiting their new home, Farley Farm in Sussex (now the home of the Lee Miller Archive) – these luminaries included Georges Braque (1882–1963), Max Ernst (1891–1976), Joan Miró (1893–1983), Picasso and Paul Éluard. This photograph was taken whilst Miller was working for *Vogue* in 1939; the curious sphinxes, a mixture of Egyptian sculpture fused with *beaux arts* figures, also appear in other fashion work she shot at the time.

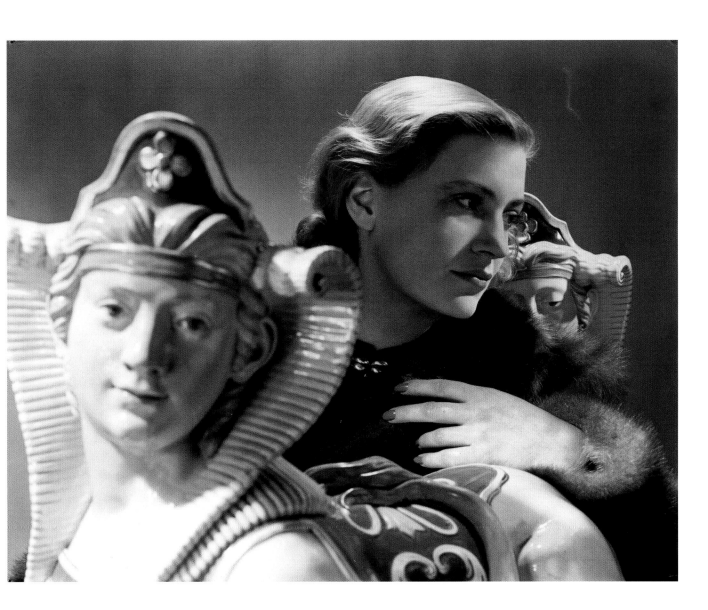

Madame Yevonde (1893–1975)
1940
Colour dye transfer print, 378 x 305mm (14⅞ x 12")
National Portrait Gallery, London (NPG P620)

This complex work represents a zany updating of the seventeenth-century genre of *vanitas* or *memento mori* painting. Yevonde, lit from behind and isolated within a gold frame, holds up a black-and-white glass negative for us to view. There is a heavy chain with keys around her neck, her right hand is encased in a plastic glove, and butterflies – symbolic of *tempus fugit* – are attached to shutter-release cords slung across the frame. This marriage of apparently haphazard and wilful organisation of space is typical of Yevonde, whose catchphrase was 'Be original or die!' This photograph was one of the last she created using the Vivex colour process (Colour Photography Limited, the firm who developed her work, did not survive World War II).

Yevonde herself was a colourful character. Born in London, she was educated in Surrey and in Belgium. In 1911 she became apprentice to Lallie Charles (see pp.46–7) and, like Dorothy Wilding (see pp.72–3), learnt the art of retouching in addition to taking photographs. In 1914 she set up on her own and from then onwards her work was published in society magazines including the *Sketch* and *Tatler*. In 1920 she married the playwright Edgar Middleton (d.1939). In 1921 she moved from 92 to 100 Victoria Street, a larger studio where she took photographs of Paul Robeson (1898–1976) and Dame Barbara Cartland (1901–2000) among other celebrities. That year she also lectured on 'Photographic Portraiture from a Woman's Point of View': 'I have tried to show that personality, tact, patience and intuition are all very valuable to the portrait photographer: that women possess them to a far greater degree than men …' Ever ready to experiment, Yevonde embraced the Vivex colour process in the 1930s and used it for her commission from *Fortune* magazine to record the grandeur of the *Queen Mary*. This included portraits of the Zinkeisen sisters at work within the ship on murals later shown at the Museum of Modern Art, New York. Yevonde is best known for her idiosyncratic series 'Goddesses' (1935), inspired by an Olympian theme party held at Claridges and consisting of society beauties dressed as Greek and Roman goddesses. For this, Yevonde let her fertile imagination run wild, and her sitters colluded to produce a remarkable, surreal and avant-garde set of images. In 1940 Yevonde's autobiography *In Camera* was published and in the 1950s she began experimenting with the solarisation process, which had been discovered by accident by Lee Miller and Man Ray in 1929 (see p.76). In 1971 she donated most of her original prints to the National Portrait Gallery.

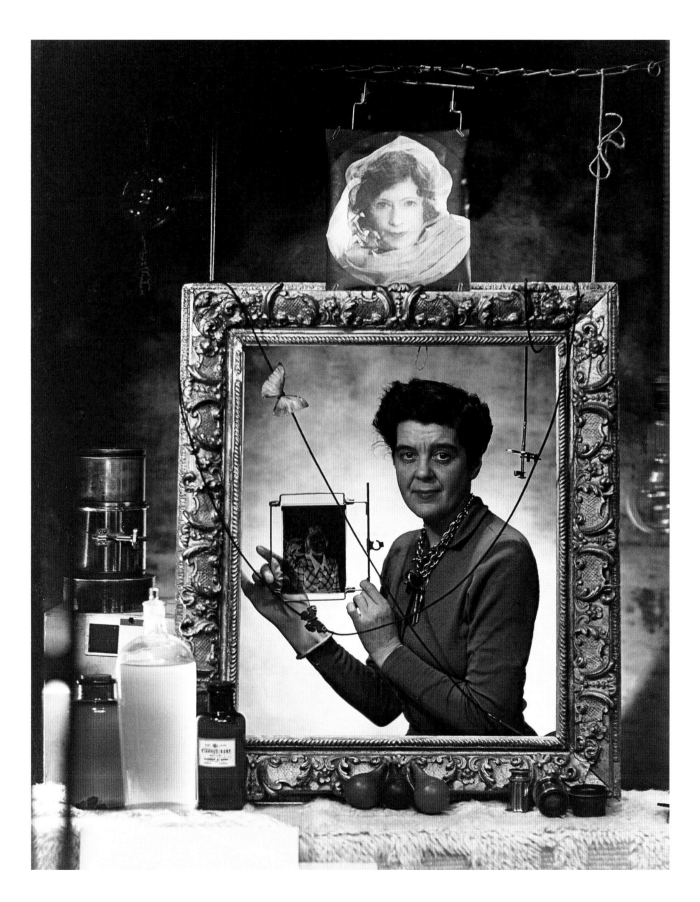

Gluck (1895–1978)
1942
Oil on canvas, 306 x 254mm (12 x 10")
National Portrait Gallery, London (NPG 6462)

Born Hannah Gluckstein into the family that founded the L. Lyons & Co. catering empire, Gluck attended classes at St John's School of Art from 1913 to 1916 and then spent time at the artist's colony at Lamorna, Cornwall. It was there that she met Laura Knight (see pp.56–7), whose studio she later bought, Ella Naper, whom she also painted, and Alfred Munnings (1878–1959), who sketched her portrait. After leaving home around 1916 she had a brief spell painting portraits of shoppers at Selfridges department store. By 1918 she was calling herself Gluck, wearing men's clothes and smoking a pipe. She is best known for her trademark 'Gluck Frame', which she patented and registered, and which she designed to fit around her paintings, making the three-tiered moulding an integral part of a room's decorative finishes. These frames were included in two major exhibitions of British Art in Industry. They were particularly popular during the 1930s when Gluck also painted the 'modern' flower arrangements created by her then lover Constance Spry (1886–1960). In 1936 Gluck painted a double profile portrait to commemorate her 'marriage' to the writer and socialite Nesta Obermer (1896–1984), entitled *Medallion*, but she referred to it as *YouWe*. This work was intended to comment on the social divisions and difficulties of leading a lesbian life at that time.

Gluck crusaded successfully for an improvement in the quality of artist's paint, lobbying for the use of cold-pressed oil and hand-ground pigments: her 'paint war' resulted in the formation of the British Standards Institution Technical Committee on Artists' Materials. Gluck also lectured on 'The impermanence of paintings in relation to artists' materials' at the Royal Society of Arts in London in 1964. She exhibited with the Fine Art Society in 1926, 1932 and 1937, and in 1973, when this portrait was acquired by the National Portrait Gallery, she wrote 'This will after all be my last one-man show and I would like to go out with a bang!' (Quoted in D. Souhami, *Gluck*, 2000, p.297.) In 1945 she moved to Steyning, Sussex, to live with the critic and journalist Edith Shackleton Heald (1885–1976), a former lover of the poet W.B. Yeats. Gluck lived there until her death in 1978. Examples of her work are in the collections of the Victoria and Albert Museum and the Smithsonian American Art Museum, Washington, DC.

Although this painting is small in scale, as was much of Gluck's work, it has tremendous presence. The artist's expression is simultaneously haughty and confident yet somehow sad and weary. The only real source of colour is a patterned kerchief – the rest is pale: white background, pasty-pink flesh tones, deep-brown eyes with matching short cropped hair. The artist's rigorous personality is implied by the clear focus on the head and the lack of flattery regarding her furrowed brow and clearly delineated lips.

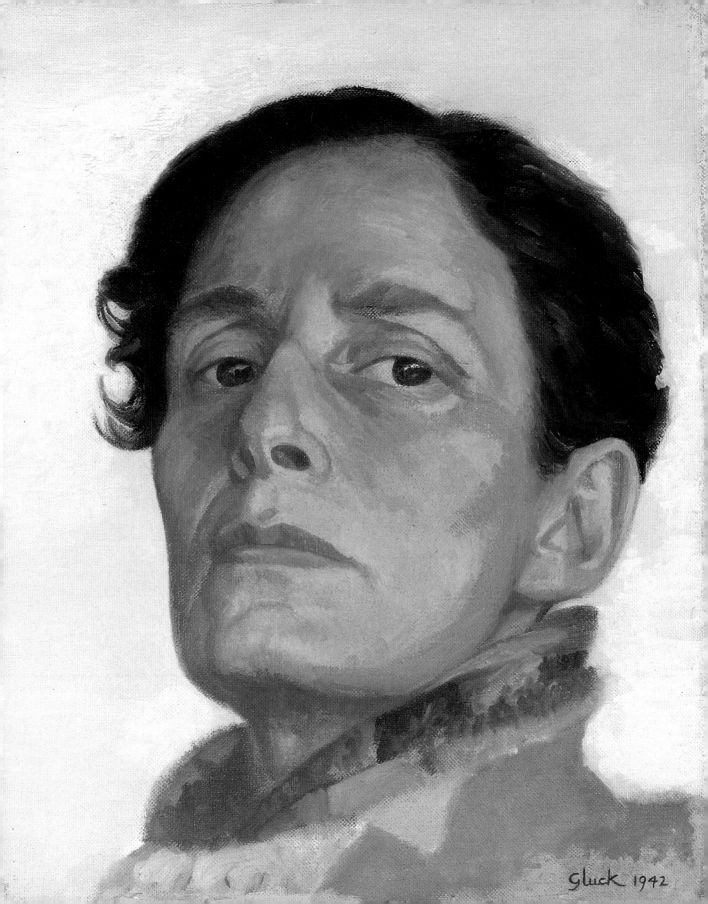
Gluck 1942

Elsie Queen (EQ) Nicholson (1908–92)

*c.*1943
Coloured inks and wax-resist crayon on paper, 484 x 410mm (19 x 16⅛")
National Portrait Gallery, London (NPG 6444)

Elsie Queen Nicholson was the granddaughter of Eveleen Myers (see pp.50–51). When she was twenty her parents moved to Leckhampton House, where EQ, as she was known, designed the interior. In 1931 she married Kit Nicholson, youngest son of the artist Sir William Nicholson (1872–1949) and Mabel Pryde. EQ had learnt the art of batik in Paris during 1926 and back in London worked in this medium for the designer Marion Dorn. EQ continued to work whilst raising her family of three, printing with lino on fabric. In 1941 she started to paint and in 1945 made designs for machine printing for Alastair Morton of Edinburgh Weavers. In 1950 she showed paintings with Keith Vaughan (1912–77) and Peter Rose Pulham (1910–56) at the Hanover Gallery and the following year her wallpapers were produced by Cole and Son. EQ gave up fabric painting at the end of the 1950s, only resuming her design activities in the 1980s when she started making rugs. Her work is in the collection of the Tate and has been compared to that of Eric Ravilious (1903–42) and Edward Bawden (1903–89), both of whom were artists and designers.

EQ was a great admirer of Braque, and there are shades of Cubism in this graphic yet dreamy work. In the lop-sided composition the glowing yellow/white head is balanced against the dark right-hand side of the page. This imbalance is underscored by the differentiation between her eyes but the effect is readjusted by the symmetry of her plaits and severe middle parting. There is a hint of a smile, almost a wink, at the viewer for being duped into thinking that portraiture is only about regular proportions. What seems simple here is in fact remarkably complex.

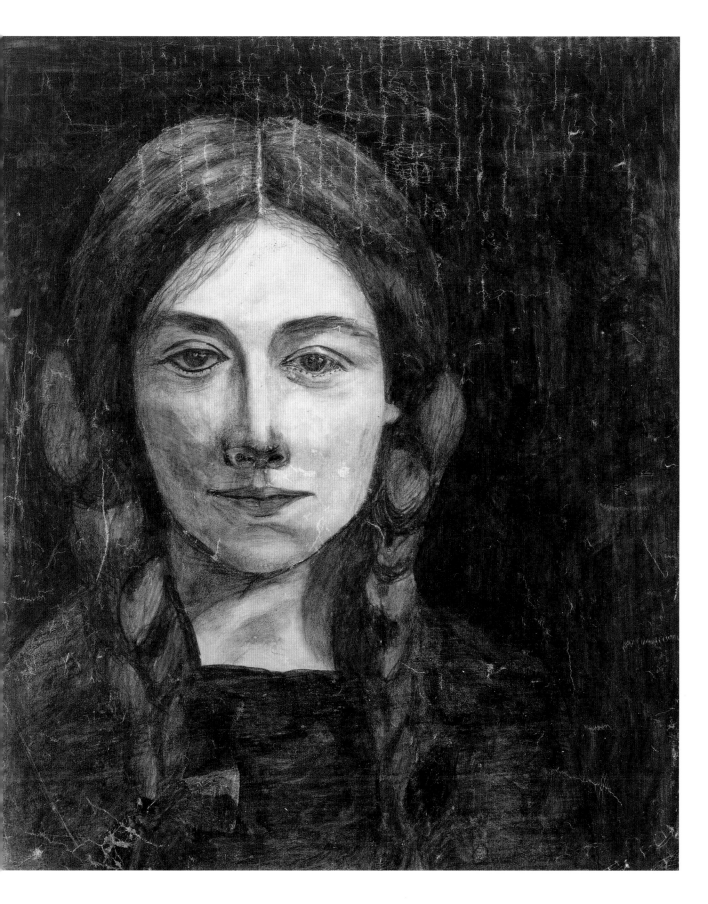

Anna Zinkeisen (1901–76)
*c.*1944
Oil on canvas, 752 x 625mm (29⅝ x 24⅝")
National Portrait Gallery, London (NPG 5884)

Anna Zinkeisen, younger sister of Doris (see pp.66–7), was born in Kilgreggan, Dunbartonshire. After attending Harrow School of Art, Anna won a scholarship to the Royal Academy, where Sir William Orpen (1878–1931) and Sir George Clausen (1852–1944) were then teaching. Orpen recommended that she transfer to the Sculpture School, which led to her designing bas-relief plaques for Wedgwood; she was the first person since John Flaxman in 1775 to provide original Wedgwood designs. Anna's three plaques won her a silver medal at the Paris Exhibition of Decorative Arts in 1925 – in 1921 she had won the Landseer Award of £40 for two years: 'You can't cast aside your great ambitions and your dreams of pure art because you work in an economic and competitive commercial world as well. The idea that the two are incompatible is all wrong.'(Quoted in J. Walpole, *'Anna' A Memorial Tribute to Anna Zinkeisen*, 1978.) Anna later specialised in pathological and clinical drawing, commenting 'It is amazing the amount of beauty one finds in horrible things like these'. With her sister Doris (as children they were known as 'Big Zinc' – Doris – and 'Little Zinc' – Anna) she painted murals on both the *Queen Mary* and *Queen Elizabeth*. During World War II she worked at St Mary's Hospital, Paddington, in the mornings nursing in the casualty ward and in the afternoons painting in a disused operating theatre. Examples of her work from this period can be seen at the Imperial War Museum, London.

This self-portrait, sharply lit from the left-hand side, draws attention to her painting arm, held in contrapposto, enhancing the impression of a confident working woman. Zinkeisen's slightly parted red lips match her sexy *décolletage*, her gaze is direct and a kiss curl hangs down above her eyebrow. Her bracelet bears the insignia of the St John's Ambulance Brigade: an enamelled Maltese Cross, the Order of St John of Jerusalem.

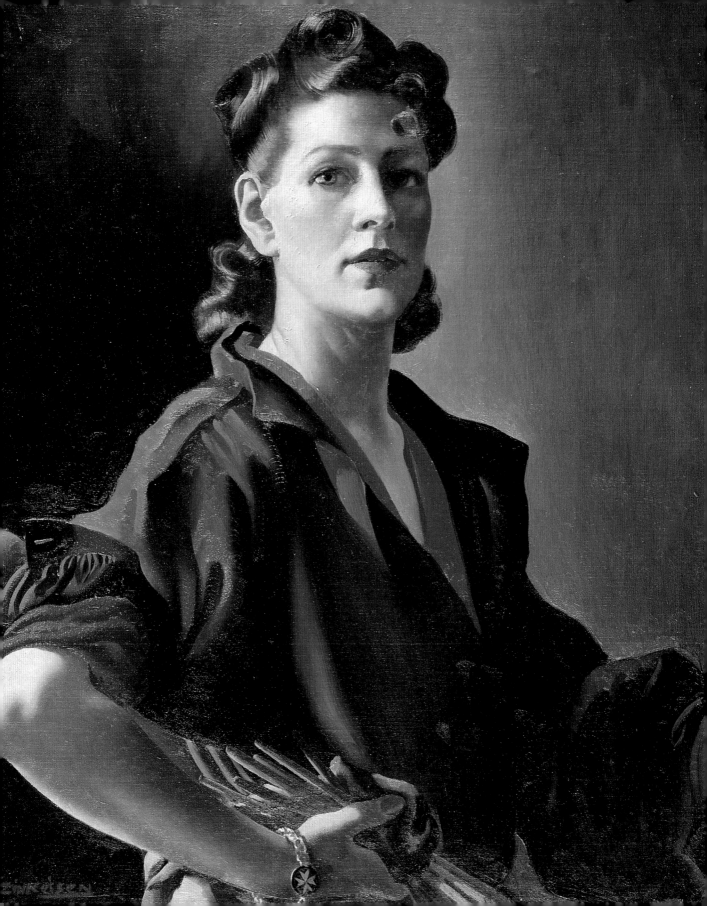

Gertrude Hermes (1901–83)
1949
Wood engraving, 203 x 152mm (8 x 6")
National Portrait Gallery, London (NPG 6002)

Born in Kent, Gertrude Hermes studied first at Beckenham School of Art from 1919 to 1921 and then at Leon Underwood's School of Painting and Sculpture between 1922 and 1926, gaining the Prix de Rome in 1925. The following year she married the artist and printmaker Blair Hughes-Stanton (1902–81), though they were divorced in 1932. She taught at the Royal Academy Schools, at St Martin's School of Art and at the Central School of Art. She became an Associate of the Royal Academy in 1963 and in 1964, together with Anne Redpath (1895–1965) and Dame Laura Knight, was invited to an Academy banquet, thus breaking a masculine tradition of 196 years. This was as a result of her letter of protest: 'No, I am not a feminist, nor have I ever felt the need to fight for rights, or anything like that. Just an artist and as such I cannot accept sex discrimination in the world of Art.' In 1971 she was elected to the Royal Academy.

Hermes designed the 9100mm (22' 10") sculptured glass window for the British Pavilion at the Paris Exposition Internationale of 1937, and was selected to represent Britain in the 1940 Venice Biennale. This was cancelled because of the outbreak of World War II, which Hermes spent in New York and Montreal with her two children. During this period she undertook war work as a draughtswoman for shipyards and aircraft factories. She exhibited widely, with the English Wood Engraving Society from 1925 to 1931, with the London Group from 1934, and at the Towner Art Gallery, Eastbourne, in 1949. She was given a retrospective at the Whitechapel Art Gallery in 1967 and at the Royal Academy in 1981. Her work can be seen in several public collections including the Tate, the British Museum, the Ashmolean Museum, Oxford, and the Whitworth Art Gallery, Manchester.

Hermes is renowned for the narrative, symbolic compositions she created in black-and-white print; she called herself a 'book decorator', but she also made sculptures in wood and bronze, receiving a medal from the Society of Portrait Sculpture in 1967. Hermes, like Dame Ethel Walker (see pp.60–61) was awarded the Order of the British Empire (1982). Constantin Brancusi (1876–1957) and Henri Gaudier-Brzeska (1891–1915) influenced her wood sculptures and one can detect their presence in this print which, with its fluid lines and play on profile/full-face, is an elegant yet simple portrait of the artist with a distinctly three-dimensional feel. Bryan Robertson, an avant-garde and respected curator who was Director of the Whitechapel Art Gallery from 1952 to 1968, remarked that Hermes' work demonstrated 'a continual and agreeable tension between sobriety and verve, classical order and sensual impulse'. (This and previous quote taken from K. Deepwell, 'Gertrude Hermes' in *Dictionary of Women Artists*, Vol. I, 1997.)

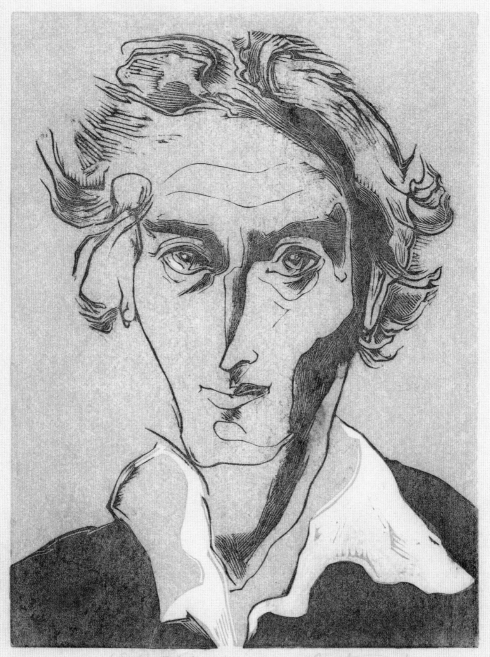

Self Portrait No 11   Gertrude Hermes
1949.

Dame Barbara Hepworth (1903–75)
1950
Oil and pencil on board, 305 x 267mm (12 x 10½")
National Portrait Gallery, London (NPG 5919)

Barbara Hepworth was born in Wakefield, Yorkshire, where her father was a civil engineer. She won a scholarship to Leeds School of Art in 1919 and there met fellow student Henry Moore, who was five years her senior. She won another scholarship to the Royal College of Art, where Sir William Rothenstein (1872–1945) was Principal. She left with a diploma in 1924 and then travelled with a scholarship to Tuscany. In Italy she married the sculptor John Skeaping (1901–80) and they returned to England in November 1926.

In 1931 Hepworth joined the Seven and Five Society whose members included Moore and Ben Nicholson, to whom Hepworth was married between 1933 and 1951. Her large sculptures were part of the British modern movement (she was especially known for her subtle use of the hole) and with them she achieved international recognition. Her work is represented in more than one hundred collections throughout the world and her studio in St Ives is now a museum. Hepworth was a pioneering sculptor in stone and wood, who thought that '...there is a whole range of formal perception belonging to feminine experience. So many ideas spring from an inside response to form.' (Quoted in P. Curtis and A.G. Wilkinson, *Barbara Hepworth: A Retrospective*, 1994–5.)

The board on which Hepworth has drawn has a thin coating of gesso. Into this the artist has made brisk pencil marks indicating the figure's hand (her own) holding the board: a classic method of self-portrayal. The surface texture is full of scratches and indentations, giving it a three-dimensional quality. In places the white is rubbed down and orange paint glows around the edges. A soft shadow is created by mixing water with the pencil on plaster. A tint of brown ink gives her hair a darker tone, while the brush strokes give it direction. These are enhanced by heavy, rhythmic swirling pencil marks to suggest individual hairs. The eyes are determinedly marked out and there is a strong highlight to the nose. The whole is a vivid, confident sketch: lively, vigorous, informal but in control.

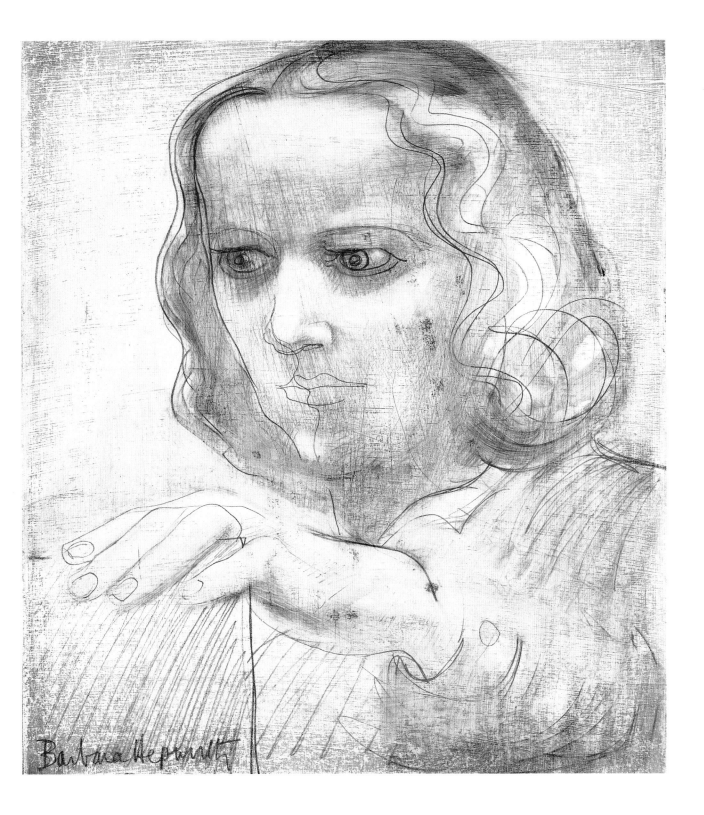

Barbara Hepworth

Elizabeth Blackadder (b.1931)
1951
Oil on canvas, 355 x 305mm (14 x 12")
Collection of the artist

Born in Falkirk, Scotland, Elizabeth Blackadder studied at Edinburgh University with Professor Talbot Rice and at Edinburgh College of Art from 1949 to 1954 under William Gillies, obtaining her MA. She taught painting there between 1962 and 1986. This painting was done at the end of her second year at Edinburgh College of Art. It has all the tentative poise of a young artist learning a trade; it is elegant and ordinary whilst it hints at the fascination with colour that later becomes so evident in her work. In scale it relates to the self-portrait by Lady Butler (see p.43) and their ages also correspond, twenty and twenty-three years old respectively.

Blackadder is best known for her fusion of oriental painting and calligraphy with Western realism. She paints flowers and still lifes in watercolour and in 1985 she visited Japan for the first time. This inspired other visits and artistic experimentation with gold leaf and large scale, scroll-like works up to 1500mm (5') long. The painter and art teacher Carel Weight (1908–97) called her pictures 'an artistic translation of her life and herself' and Judith Bumpus, author of a monograph on Blackadder's work, commented on their 'precision and vitality'. Blackadder's portrait of Lady Naomi Mitchison of 1988 is in the National Portrait Gallery's collection and was selected by the Labour Government for show at No. 10 Downing Street. In 1995, like Dorothy Wilding (see pp.72–3), the Royal Mail used her work for a set of stamps. She became a member of the Royal Academy in 1976 and in 1982 was awarded the Order of the British Empire. In 2001 she was appointed Her Majesty's Painter and Limner in Scotland. Her work can be found in the collections of many major institutions including the Tate, the Scottish National Portrait Gallery, the Government Art Collection, the Museum of Modern Art, New York, and the Scottish National Gallery of Modern Art, where she had a solo show in 1999.

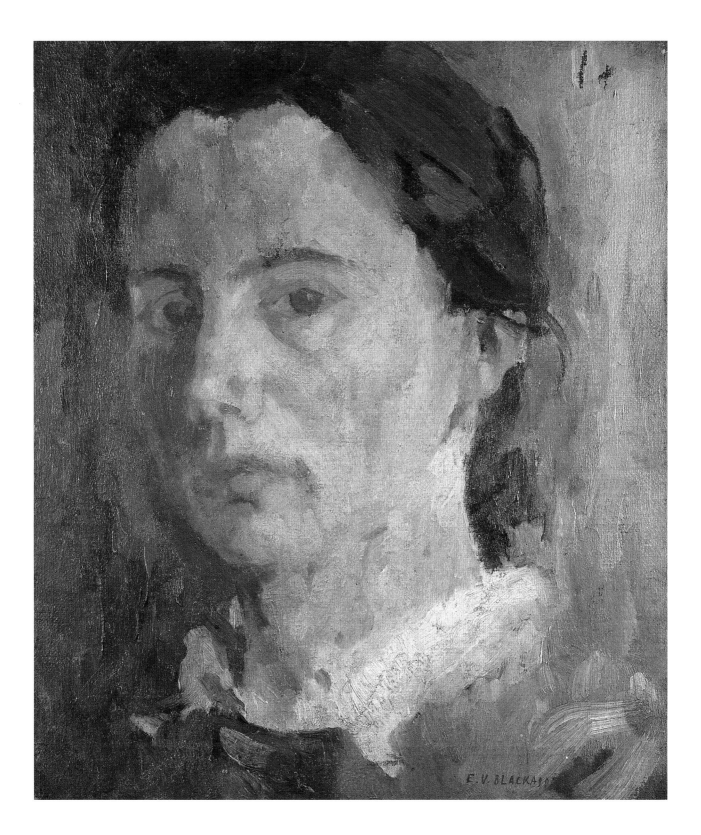

Marie-Louise von Motesiczky (1906–96)
Self-portrait in black, 1959
Oil and pastel on canvas, 1050 x 590mm (41⅜ x 23¼")
Marie-Louise von Motesiczky Charitable Trust

Marie-Louise von Motesiczky was born in Vienna but left with her mother after the Anschluss (the annexation of Austria by Nazi Germany) in 1938, spending a year in Holland before coming to England in 1939. They spent the war years in Amersham, Buckinghamshire, where they mixed with fellow *émigrés* Oskar Kokoschka (1886–1980), whom they had known previously in Vienna, and Elias Canetti (1905–94), with whom von Motesiczky later had a long affair. Mother and daughter settled in Hampstead after the war.

At eighteen von Motesiczky was in Paris studying at the Montparnasse Painting Academy, and between 1927 and 1928 she studied at Max Beckmann's (1884–1950) master class in the Städel School in Frankfurt. Beckmann is said to have told her that she could be the successor to Paula Modersohn-Becker, who had died in 1907. This self-portrait, although painted about thirty years later, bears witness to the distinctive use of black in Beckmann's Expressionist style. Von Motesiczky portrays herself in a dark cocktail dress, the yellow spots and rivulets of turpentine on the surface of the painting catching the light and making an abstract rhythm with the glowing backdrop of the yellow-ochre door. The large amber-coloured necklace repeats the colour and shape of her hair. Her pose is vaguely reminiscent of that of Gwen John (see p.49), but the awkwardly painted left arm, which appears crammed within the dramatic and severe black framework, seems to hint at a feeling of claustrophobia.

Von Motesiczky's painting career spanned seventy years. She produced still lifes, landscapes, allegorical works and portraits, among which are several intense self-portraits. She also painted many touching images of her mother in various guises – in her three-wheeled electric car and smoking her pipe. Von Motesiczky's first show was in The Hague in January 1939, followed by the exhibition *Continental Art* at the Leger Gallery in 1941, and with the sculptor Mary Dumas at the Czechoslovak Institute in 1944. Helen Lessore (1907–94) gave her a solo show at the Beaux Arts Gallery, London, in 1960. Her work is in the collections of the Tate, the Stedelijk Museum of Modern Art, Amsterdam, and the Historisches Museum der Stadt Wien, Austria.

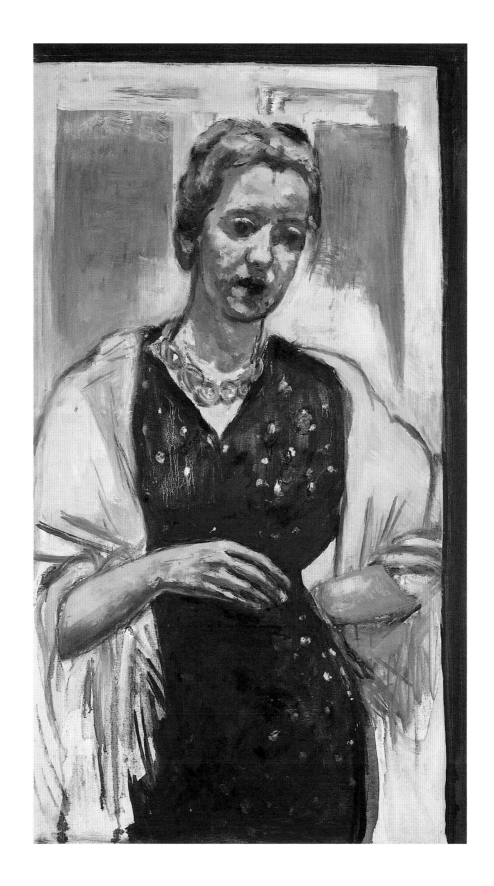

Ida Kar (1907–74)

*c.*1960
Modern print from a 2¼" square film negative, 203 x 152mm (8 x 6")
National Portrait Gallery, London (NPG x88688)

Born in Tambov, Russia, Ida Kar spent her childhood in Russia and Iran until her parents moved to Egypt when she was thirteen. In Alexandria she attended the Lycée Français and at twenty went to Paris to study medicine and chemistry. These subjects were exchanged for singing and violin as Kar was swept up in the excitement of Paris, left-wing politics, and the artistic avant-garde. On her return to Egypt in 1933 she began working in a photographic studio. She married Edmond Belali, a keen amateur photographer and Egyptian government official, and they moved to Cairo where they set up their own studio called 'Idabel'. At around this time Lee Miller (see pp.76–7) was in Egypt too, and it is interesting to speculate on whether she might have been an influence on the work that Kar and her husband showed in the two Surrealist exhibitions they contributed to in 1943–4. Certainly Victor Musgrave (1919–84), a British artist, curator and critic, took notice and in 1944 Kar divorced Belali, married Musgrave and moved to London. Here she began to specialise in photographing artists and writers who were part of London's Soho scene. In 1954 she exhibited images of *Forty Artists from Paris and London*. In 1957 the *Observer* commissioned her to take photographs in Armenia, where she turned her attention to the rural communities, and this series of photographs gave her work a new focus. Three years later she showed at the Whitechapel Art Gallery – the first ever solo photography exhibition at a major art gallery in London – exhibiting black-and-white portraits of artists including Germaine Richier (1904–59), Sandra Blow (b.1925), Alberto Giacometti (1901–66), George Braque and Man Ray. Also included were examples of some of her work from Armenia and Russia. The exhibition was a resounding success, receiving much press attention.

This self-portrait dates from that period and has an upbeat, contemporary feel. Kar liked to photograph her sitters at home or in the studio using natural light, and here we see her staring at us, her body balanced somewhat awkwardly on a minimalist wooden kitchen surface. The strong illumination creates dramatic chiaroscuro and, with the angles created by the corner of the room, forces the attention of the viewer to the centre of the image where Kar holds in pride of place her Roliflex camera. There is a satisfying simplicity to this work, an openness to recording the bare bones of the situation: the light, the camera, the person. Kar's work improved the status of photography in Britain, and her documentation of artists is a valuable resource. This portrait is part of her archive, which is held at the National Portrait Gallery.

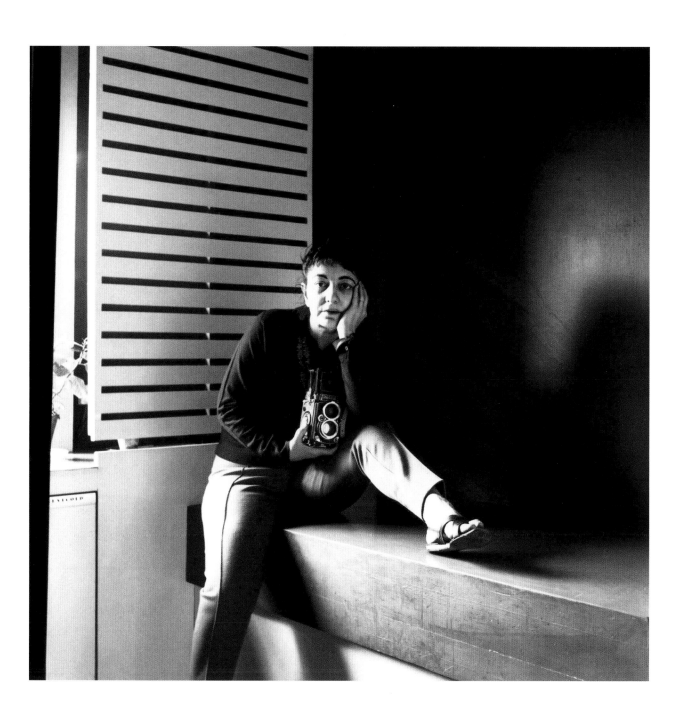

Maggi Hambling (b.1945)
1977–8
Oil on canvas, 1520 x 1750mm (59⅞ x 68⅞")
National Portrait Gallery, London (NPG 6562)

Maggi Hambling studied with the artists Arthur Lett-Haines (1894–1978) and Cedric Morris (1889–1982) at the East Anglian School of Painting and Drawing from 1960 and then at Ipswich School of Art (1962–4), Camberwell (1964–7) and the Slade (1967–9). In 1969 she won a Boise Travel Award and in 1977 an Arts Council of England award. She was the first Artist in Residence at the National Gallery (1980–81) and was joint winner (with Patrick Caulfield) of the Jerwood Prize for Painting in 1995.

    This portrait was presented to the National Portrait Gallery by Imperial Tobacco Ltd in 1992 – appropriately, as in it Hambling smokes a cigarette, one of three life essentials (according to her) together with a drink and paintbrushes. The portrait concerns what Hambling called the 'muddle of life'. The artist confronts us with her dilemma; spiritually she is in love with the person who made the teapot, physically she is in love with the person we glimpse in the lower right-hand corner of the canvas.

> I may do a self-portrait when I am not obsessed with painting another person. I don't choose my obsessions; they choose me. Someone or something moves me, and that's how it happens. When I am painting someone else, I try to empty myself so the truth can come through me on to the canvas or into the bronze. I try to be a channel.
> (*Independent on Sunday*, 1 August 1999)

Hambling has made series of works inspired by bullfights, sunrises and laughter and more recently she produced the monument to Oscar Wilde installed behind St Martin-in-the-Fields in 1998. She is a vivid public figure, speaking out in favour of camp and recently against the erosion of art schools. She has had solo exhibitions at the Serpentine Gallery, National Gallery, National Portrait Gallery (*Pictures of Max Wall*), Yale Center for British Art and Marlborough Fine Art. Her portrait of Professor Dorothy Hodgkin (1985), winner of the 1964 Nobel Prize for Chemistry, is a favourite in the collection of the National Portrait Gallery. Her works are in numerous public collections including the Tate, National Gallery and British Museum.

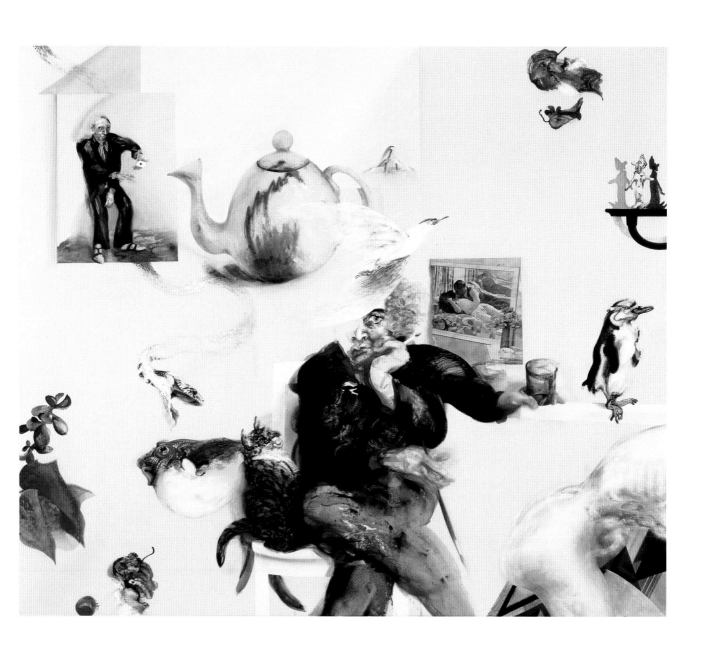

Glenys Barton (b.1944)

Lady with Three Faces, 1980
Ceramic (polished bone china and marble), height 432mm (17")
Flowers East, London

Glenys Barton was born in the Potteries' capital, Stoke-on-Trent. Her mother was briefly a 'paintress' (a hand-painter on china; see p.74) and her aunts worked as professional pottery gilders all their lives. Barton first studied to be a teacher in Bristol, where she says she 'did pottery all the time', before going to the Royal College of Art to study ceramics between 1968 and 1971. Exposure to what she describes as 'the shock of art' at the RCA confirmed her commitment to making unique artworks in ceramic.

In 1976 she spent eighteen months 'in residence' at the Josiah Wedgwood Factory, Stoke-on-Trent, refining her knowledge of the properties and possibilities of bone china as a medium for making sculpture. This resulted in twenty-six works that were exhibited in London and New York. Since that time she has hardly used bone china, excepting this self-portrait which is one of an edition of eight. In his catalogue for her exhibition at the National Portrait Gallery in 1997 Robin Gibson wrote perceptively about the nature of this work:

> The self-portrait is a discipline often chosen by young artists as a means of self-examination at a time of insecurity – doubts about the face which they must present to the world and the direction which they and their art intend to take. It is therefore somehow reassuring that Barton also felt compelled at the beginning of the eighties to undertake this exercise, thereby producing her earliest portrait work.

Barton's self-portrait is full of clarity and calm, the elegant figure poised and ready to choose any one of the three masks. This concept of the multiple persona is reiterated in the portrait by Jennifer McRae (see p.109); in Barton's piece, however, the cool hardness and fragility of the material employed produce a distancing effect, added to which the figure itself has no face at all – a blank surface.

Barton has exhibited widely in the United Kingdom and abroad. Her work is held in many public collections including the Boymans Museum, Rotterdam, the National Museum of Victoria, Melbourne, the Victoria and Albert Museum, the Scottish National Portrait Gallery and the National Portrait Gallery.

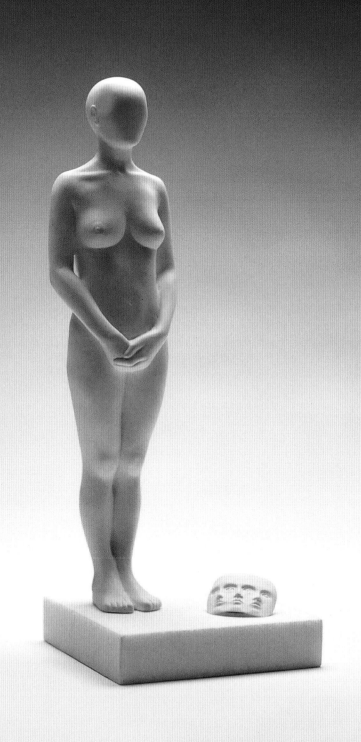

Helen Chadwick (1953–96)
Vanitas II, 1986
Cibachrome print, 509 x 509mm (20 x 20")
National Portrait Gallery, London (NPG P874)

Trained at Croydon, Brighton and Chelsea College of Art (MA, 1977), Helen Chadwick is known for her provocative work concerning the body. This *vanitas* self-portrait was shown and selected for the National Museum of Film, Photography and Television Sun-Life awards in 1987. It was made as a companion piece to her installation entitled *Of Mutability*, shown at the Institute of Contemporary Arts in 1986 and can be seen here reflected in the mirror. (The actual photograph was taken by her long-term photographic collaborator, Edward Woodman, b.1943.) To create this installation she obtained sponsorship for a photocopier, making hundreds of copies of objects ranging from a dead lamb (obtained from her brother, a Sussex shepherd), to flowers and fish, including images of herself in acrobatic positions. The blue photocopies were cut and collaged together to make compositions with her as protagonist, a lyrical, sensual mermaid, and these were arranged with a set of five golden balls. Chadwick used the photo-booth installed at the National Portrait Gallery in the summer of 1985 to make the crying heads that form the tops of the computer-designed paper columns, created with the help of her then partner, architect Philip Stanley (b.1950), and acquired technical help for her 'golden ball' production from the National Portrait Gallery's frame conservation department. 'The sphere is an idealised form,' she said

> Here they represent fingertips exploded as spheres. Gold is a material which had associations with the eternal – purity, value – setting up a contrast with the transience of the photocopied imagery ... Although [*Of Mutability*] plays on the decorative aspects of the rococo, it's eminently flat. The stucco has lost all sense of relief, it has become a succession of reprographic marks on a flat vertical or horizontal surface.
> (S. Baptiste and N. Wegner, eds., *Interviews with the Artists*, 1992)

Chadwick continued to court notoriety with her exuberant work, in particular a set of bronze sculptures called 'Piss Flowers', the moulds of which were made by urinating in the snow whilst she was on a residency in Banff, Canada. These gained wide public interest when exhibited at the Serpentine Gallery in 1994. Chadwick was also an influential lecturer and was nominated for the Turner Prize in 1987. Her work is in the collections of the Victoria and Albert Museum, the Tate, the European Parliament, and the British Council.

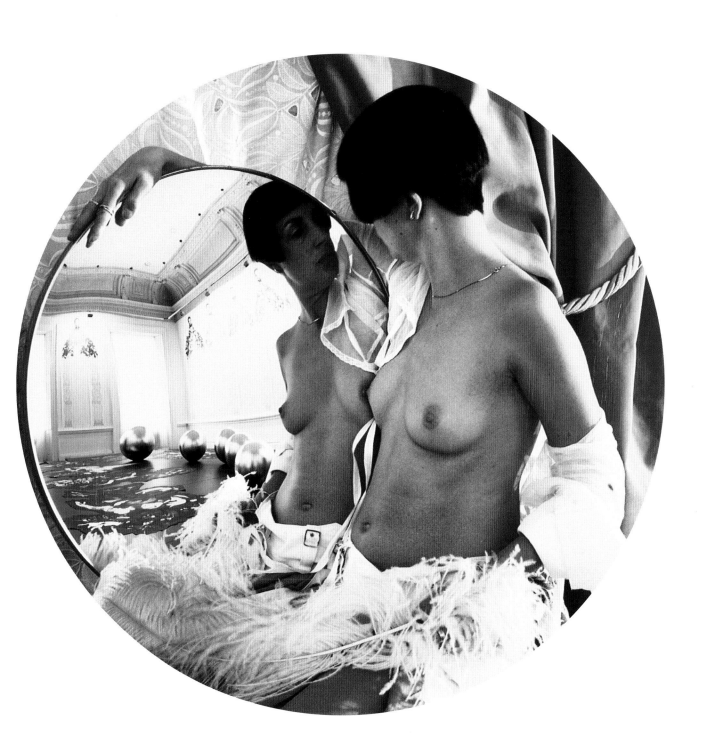

Jo Spence (1934–92)
1990
Colour print, 409 x 285mm (16⅛ x 11¼")
National Portrait Gallery, London (NPG P849)

Born Joan Patricia Clode to working-class parents in London, Jo Spence left school for secretarial college aged thirteen. She started work when she was fifteen and from 1951 to 1962 was secretary at a commercial photography studio in Finchley Road. This led her to join the Hampstead Camera Club. After a short-lived marriage in 1965, she went to Ireland with Neil Spence, whose name she adopted, and on her return she set up a studio in Hampstead, Joanna Spence Associates, which specialised in portraiture, weddings and actors' portfolios. In 1972 Spence helped set up the Children's Rights Workshop and with an Arts Council grant produced her exhibition *Children Photographed*.

In 1974 she met the photographer and alternative educationalist Terry Dennett (b.1938), and together they set up the independent teaching organisation Photography Workshop Ltd (1974–92), which was responsible for helping to initiate a number of projects including the Hackney Flashers Women's Photography Group that created two important photo-projects, 'Women and Work' and 'Who's Holding the Baby?' In 1979 she participated in the Hayward Gallery exhibition *Three Perspectives on Photography*. In 1982, with Dennett, she produced *Remodelling Photo History*. That same year she gained First Class Honours in the Theory and Practice of Photography at the Polytechnic of Central London, and in November was diagnosed with breast cancer. This crisis provoked Spence to develop her own self-medication, which included the use of photography as a therapeutic alternative to drugs. From 1983 she collaborated with the photographer Rosy Martin (b.1946), and together they coined the term 'phototherapy'. Spence's autobiography, *Putting Myself in the Picture* (1986), describes phototherapy as meaning 'quite literally, using photography to heal ourselves'. Her final book, *Cultural Sniping: The Art of Transgression*, was edited and published posthumously in 1995. Her work is now held in the Jo Spence Memorial Archive, London.

Spence went on to collaborate with various people including her partner David Roberts, whom she later married. This portrait emerged from a 1989 phototherapy session with Dr Tim Sheard from the Bristol Cancer Help Centre. It was originally the central image in a triptych used for the poster that advertised the exhibition *Missing Persons/Damaged Lives* at Leeds City Art Gallery in 1991. In the photograph Spence confronts us, appearing grotesque, her face behind a hag-like mask. Armed with a dagger and a shield, she is both scary and comic. The inclusion of an assortment of chocolates undercuts a more sombre interpretation of the work and refers to eating obsessions. 'She challenged the myth of the body beautiful, while acknowledging its power. Admitting her terror, she confronted the phantasmagoria of disease.' (Obituary, *Independent*, 25 June 1992.)

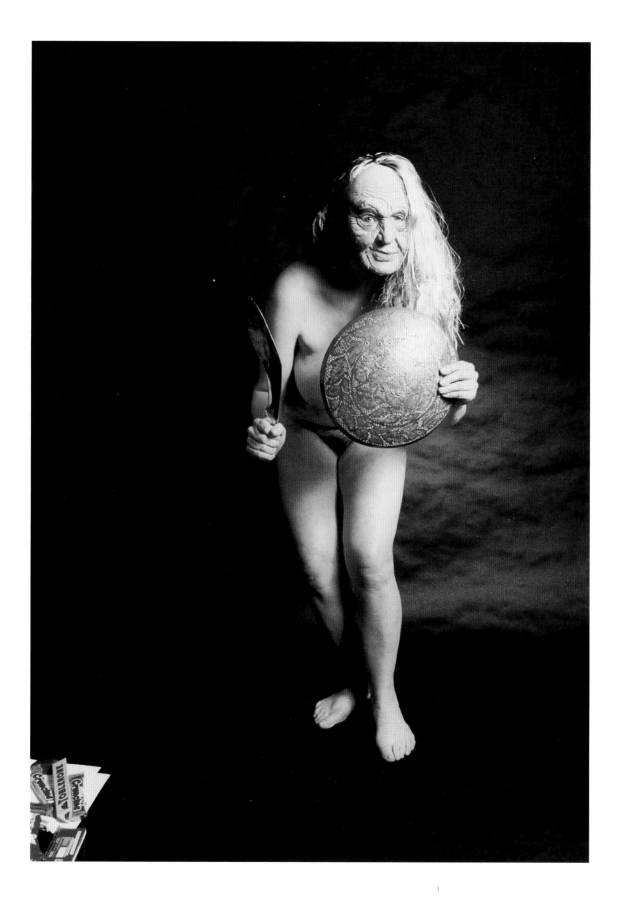

Victoria Crowe (b.1945)
Italian Reflections, 1993
Oil on board, 735 x 890mm (29 x 35")
Collection of the artist

Born in Kingston upon Thames, Surrey, Victoria Crowe studied at art college there between 1961 and 1965, followed by the Royal College of Art from 1965 to 1968. Between 1968 and 1998 she lectured in painting and drawing at Edinburgh College of Art.

In her self-portrait *Italian Reflections* Crowe introduces us to a number of her painting themes. Out of the window we view an Umbrian landscape in perspective, the cypresses making strong verticals which echo those that carve up the spaces in the portrait. Anchoring the work is a child – lying on its back and almost pinioned by a thin column bearing the profile of the angel also seen to the right of this symbolically loaded painting. The baby appears as if in parenthesis, representing the art of Piero della Francesca (*c*.1415–92) and all Renaissance babies. Strangely this work seems to prefigure the tragic events that befell Victoria Crowe some two years later, when her son died aged twenty-two from cancer. The artist is solemn, staring at us, provoking us to analyse this complex narrative. The shadow is on the child, and the light falls on the landscape and the open bowl, which sits in resplendent isolation. The painting is bathed in Siennese brown, with the exception of the yellow light and the smallest strip of vibrant sky blue. It is a visual essay on the possibilities of the aesthetic balancing act: light, form and pattern. There is a certain spiritual dimension mixed with a strong autobiographical presence, which gives her work pathos and conviction.

Crowe is a regular exhibitor at the Royal Academy, the Royal Scottish Academy and the Royal Scottish Society of Painters in Watercolour. She has long been involved in wildlife conservation projects through 'Artists for Nature'. Her work is held in many public collections including the National Portrait Gallery, the Contemporary Art Society, the Scottish National Gallery of Modern Art, the Royal Academy, the Royal College of Art and the Scottish National Portrait Gallery, where in 2000 she had a major exhibition of portraits of a Scottish shepherdess, Jenny Armstrong, entitled *A Shepherd's Life*.

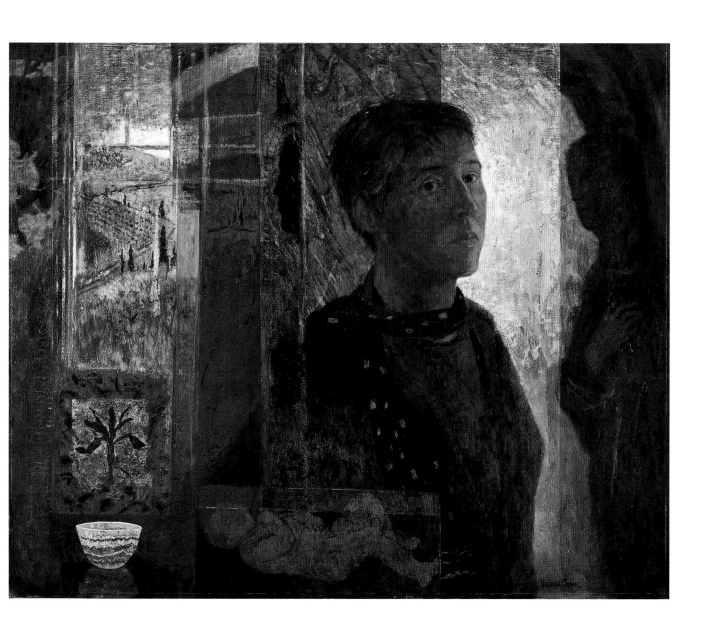

Deanna Petherbridge (b.1939)
Portrait of the Artist: Double Vision, 2000–2001
Pen and ink wash on paper, 764 x 570mm (30⅛ x 22½")
Collection of the artist

Petherbridge comments on this work:

> This recent self-portrait is concerned with the gaze and with feminist issues of ageing. Looking at myself looking has involved speculation about spectacles: how they both enhance and obscure vision. The drawing employs the historical trope of a female personification of art with her mouth bound with a ribbon: the traditional emblem of art as 'dumb poetry'. Like other aspects of this drawing, this can be interpreted as a *double entendre*: the reason for the title of the work.

Deanna Petherbridge is an artist who has worked in the medium of pen and ink on paper since the late 1960s, producing very large drawings or small works in series. These are often related to architectonic imagery and social and political themes. Her huge oil and stippled mural on the curved drum-wall of the Concert Hall in Birmingham's International Convention Centre is painted on four floors and visible from outside the building. Petherbridge has designed for ballet at the Royal Opera House and Sadler's Wells. She is a writer, critic and teacher and has published widely on issues related to art and architecture, including public art and drawing. She also curates exhibitions including the South Bank Centre's National Touring Exhibition *The Primacy of Drawing: An Artist's View* in 1991, and in 1997 the Hayward Gallery's National Touring Exhibition *The Quick and the Dead: Artists and Anatomy*. She is Professor of Drawing at the Royal College of Art, where she runs the Centre for Drawing Research, and is currently completing a large-scale book on issues related to the practice, theory and pedagogy of historical and contemporary drawing. Petherbridge was awarded a CBE in 1996. Her drawings are in public collections and she has exhibited internationally, with extensive British Council tours in India and Southeast Asia.

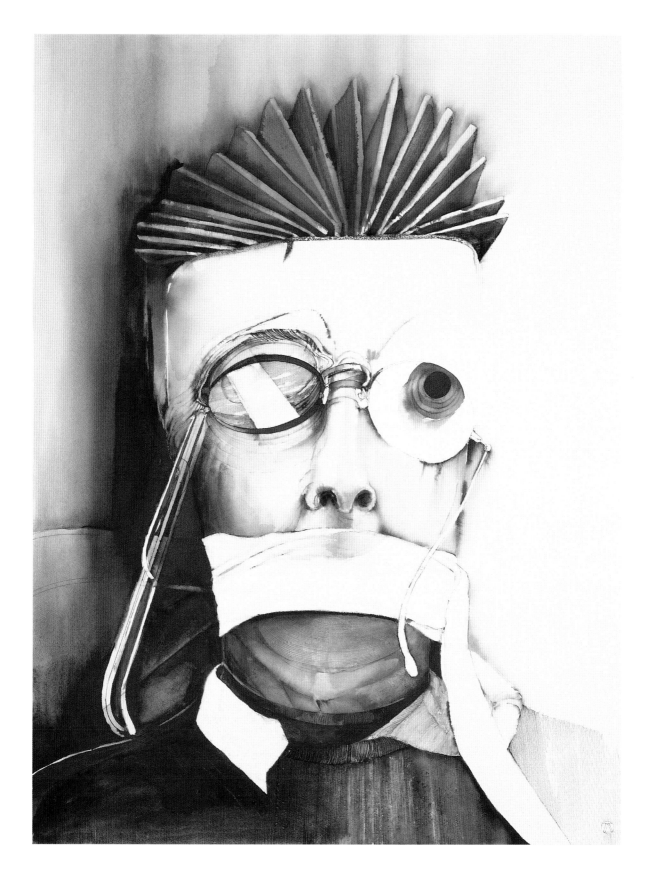

Jennifer McRae (b.1959)
Double Exposure, 2001
Oil on canvas, 840 x 1270mm (33 x 50")
Collection of the artist

Cheshire-born, Jennifer McRae has divided her working life between Glasgow and London. She studied at Gray's School of Art, Aberdeen, where she later taught in the painting department for two years. She now paints full time. Her work has been exhibited throughout Britain and in the United States of America.

Included five times in the BP Portrait Award, in 1999 she won the Travel Award and spent November of that year at the Hogeschool Sint-Lukas, Brussels, an art school specialising in drawing and painting from the figure. Her time in Belgium was spent making portraits of both staff and students, and a display of this work was held at the National Portrait Gallery concurrent with the BP Portrait Award 2000.

McRae has said 'Whenever I start a new body of work, I always start with myself, just to break the ice', and this self-portrait, like that of Daphne Todd (see p.111), deals with issues of duality within one's persona, and how one is perceived. Here McRae presents a staring full-face portrait beside an identically dressed portrait with downcast eyes. These are separated by the seemingly identical halves of a pear, also in shifting orientation – the same but not the same. The artist made these comments about the work: 'I've always felt a sense of dichotomy with the "self" and have always believed a human being is made up of personae rather than just one personality.' The use of vibrant orange echoes the self-portrait of Dame Laura Knight (see p.57) and also that of *Self-portrait with a Sunflower* by Sir Anthony van Dyck (1632–3; in the collection of the Duke of Westminster); the vivid colour arrests our attention and dominates this cleverly balanced and engineered composition. The asymmetrical pear halves draw attention to the two differing poses which in turn reiterate the multiple layers of an individual's personality.

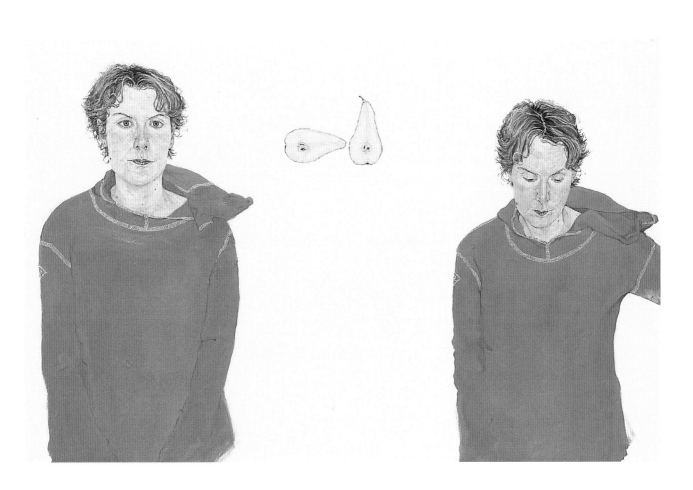

Daphne Todd (b.1947)
Me in a magnifying mirror, 2001
Oil on skin plywood, 410 x 410mm (16⅛ x 16⅛")
Collection of the artist

Daphne Todd was born in Yorkshire and studied at the Slade School of Fine Art under Sir William Coldstream (1908–87) from 1964 to 1971. Whilst there she was awarded the British Institute Award for Figurative Painting, the Tonks Drawing Prize and the intercollegiate David Murray Award for landscape painting. She exhibited at the Royal Academy from 1969 onwards and taught at the Byam Shaw and the Heatherley Schools of Art. In 1984 she was elected a member of the New English Art Club and in 1985 of the Royal Society of Portrait Painters. She has exhibited widely in the United Kingdom, including winning first prize in the Hunting/*Observer* Award in 1984, second prize in 1983 for the John Player Portrait Award, and exhibiting solo in 1989 at the Morley Gallery, London. In 1994 Daphne Todd was elected the first woman president of the Royal Society of Portrait Painters, an office she held for six years. (The Society was founded in 1891 and past presidents include Sir William Orpen, Sir John Lavery and Augustus John.)

Todd has often been preoccupied with the framing of the subject within the space of the picture plane, as in her portrait of the tall figure of Christopher Ondaatje in the National Portrait Gallery's collection, caught (almost jammed) within the doorway of his library. In her self-portrait the round magnifying mirror acts as a centralising device separating the various aspects of her life: outside the sunset of a Sussex landscape and the watery pools of her farm, and inside the abstract colours of the interior space. The splitting of this painting into four parts suggests the juggling of the different parts of life – the 'real' (outdoor, outer, physical) versus the 'abstract' (inside, internal, cerebral). It is a bold and knowing work, specific, powerful, complex yet modest in scale. It is typical in palette, with the familiar and strange mixtures of oranges with pinks and indigo/violets that have become her trademark. Todd has work in many public collections including the Science Museum, the Royal Academy (Chantrey Bequest), the Royal Holloway Museum and Art Gallery, and Oxford and Cambridge Universities.

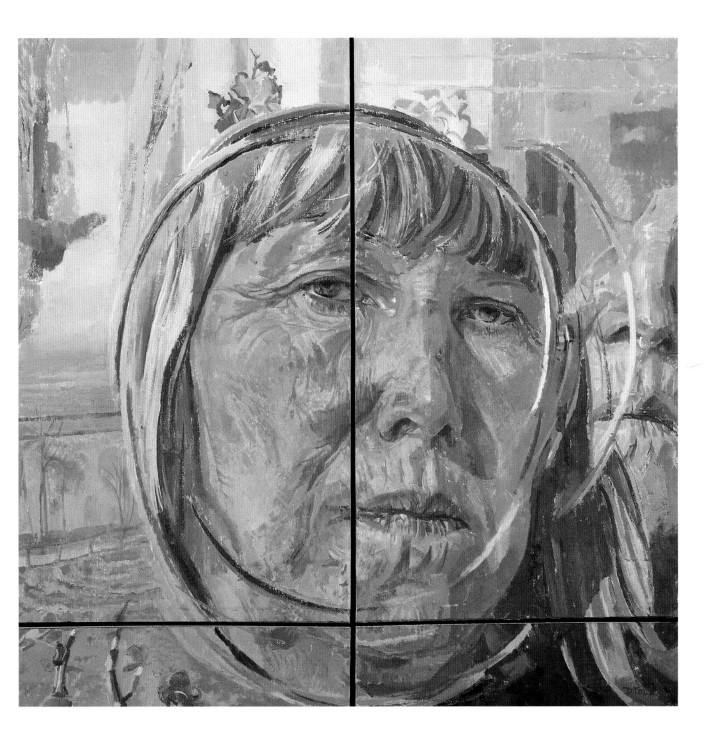

Nicola Hicks (b.1960)
2001
Charcoal on brown paper, 1300 x 1270mm (51⅛ x 50")
Collection of the artist

Nicola Hicks attended Chelsea School of Art (1978–82) and then the Royal College of Art (1982–85). A sculptor interested primarily in modelling rather than carving, Hicks has developed her own particular method of using plaster together with straw as a medium. This allows her to work with both a sense of speed and malleability. She also continues to use charcoal and brown paper to make her working drawings. Hicks has made several site-specific works, sometimes using only mud and straw, for example *Mother and Child* at the Yorkshire Sculpture Park and *The Fields of Akeldama* in Ireland. More recently she made a *Rhinoceros Beetle* for the Bristol Science Park and a monument for the Inner Temple courtyard, London. These permanent pieces, together with those on view at the Hakone Open-air Museum, Japan, and in Battersea Park, London, confirm her status as a sculptor. Yet whilst reaffirming this traditional figurative mode, she is nonetheless an artist who is interested in combining the old-fashioned with the contemporary – the past and the present – within her work. This insistence on using what might usually be termed base or cheap materials to create three-dimensional hybrid mythical forms is typical of a determination to embrace rawness, and to combine this with direct observation from life. Recently she has moved out of London to the Lake District to enjoy a studio as big as that used by the famous animal painter George Stubbs (1724–1806), where she can work directly from nature and draw sheep and horses from life.

Hicks has travelled the world for inspiration for her work and has exhibited in India, Japan, North America and Europe. Her solo exhibitions have been at the Whitworth Art Gallery, Manchester, the Yorkshire Sculpture Park, Wakefield, the Ferens Art Gallery, Hull, and the Glasgow Museum of Modern Art. Her work can be found in many collections including the Castle Museum, Norwich, the Contemporary Art Society and the Glasgow Museum of Modern Art.

Here, Hicks has used her preferred medium of charcoal on brown paper. The central mass of outdoor clothes gives an impression of a swaddled figure ready to brave the elements. Only the head is exposed, the expression determined, confident yet pensive. The woollen hat has horn-like knitted stumps that project outwards, reminiscent of the works she has made which merge the characteristics of animals and humans.

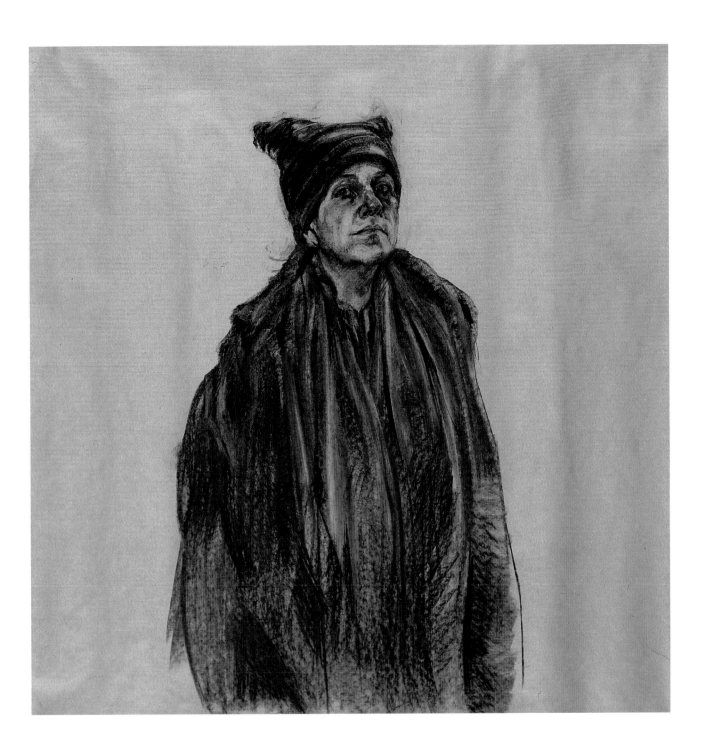

Yolanda Sonnabend (b.1935)
2001
Oil on canvas, 760 x 519mm (29⅞ x 20⅜")
Collection of the artist

Born in Zimbabwe, Yolanda Sonnabend has lived in England since 1954. She studied at the Académie des Beaux-Arts, Geneva, in 1951 and then at the Slade School of Fine Art from 1955 to 1960, studying stage design under Robert Medley (1905–94). Her first stage design for Covent Garden was for Sir Peter Wright's ballet *A Blue Rose* with music by Samuel Barber, and she received a Boise Travel Award in 1960. She was visiting tutor in stage design at the Central School of Art, Camberwell School of Art and Wimbledon School of Art, and since 1990 she has been a lecturer at the Slade. Her work has been primarily for ballet, including *Swan Lake* produced by Anthony Dowell in 1984 for the Royal Ballet. Her most important collaborations have been at Covent Garden with the late Sir Kenneth Macmillan (1929–92). She has designed for the opera and theatre, most recently for the Royal Shakespeare Theatre (*Camino Real* and *Antony and Cleopatra*). Her work has included designs for cinema, notably for Derek Jarman's (1942–94) *The Tempest*, and also for television. Sonnabend was given a British Council grant in 1979 to study baroque theatre in Prague, and in 1979 an Arts Council bursary to research mask-making in Geneva. She has worked in Europe and America, also creating installations in Denmark and Japan. Her painting has been shown in one-person exhibitions at the Whitechapel Art Gallery in 1975 and at the Serpentine Gallery in 1986.

The National Portrait Gallery's collection includes her painting of her former colleague Sir Kenneth Macmillan and an emotionally gripping portrait of Professor Stephen Hawking (b.1942). Sonnabend's arresting portrait of Hawking is as tragic as it is beautiful. She makes a magical fusion between his disability (he suffers from motor neurone disease) and his genius. Her self-portrait, which is painted on an old canvas (and incorporates to some extent the previous composition) shows her emerging from the rubble of chaos, and in some ways symbolises her strength and stubborn resilience. She has survived the vagaries and difficulties of an artistic career, and is still vigorously making art the centre of her life. For her 1986 Serpentine show she wrote the following:

Paint and canvas impose a certain simplicity, and ideas from the theatre encourage me to focus on the subject, not the image. Theatre design experiments, manipulates, plays with quotation, reference, style and pastiche and perhaps I counterbalance this by directness in painting, and resistance to building up surface texture on the canvas (which I like to keep smooth). So there is always a tension between the two activities … Traditionally, painting and designing have been seen as alternatives. I believe that it is possible and fruitful to be equally committed to both.

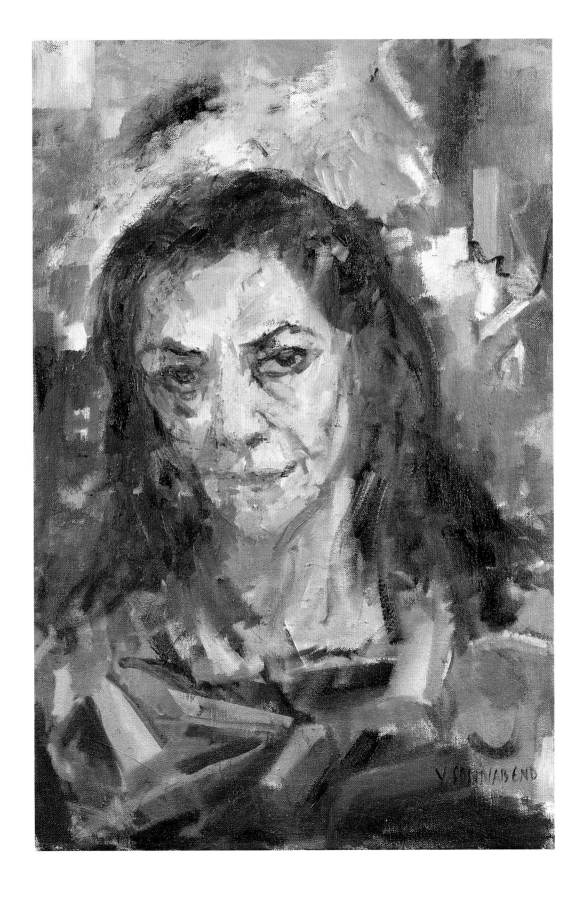

Select bibliography

C. Baile de Laperriere, *The Society of Women Artists Exhibitors 1855–1996*, Volumes I to IV (Hilmarton Manor Press, Wiltshire, 1996)

R. Betterton, *Looking On: Images of Femininity in the Visual Arts and Media* (Pandora Press, London and New York, 1987)

F. Borzello, *Seeing Ourselves: women's self-portraits* (Thames and Hudson, London, 1998)

—, *A World of Our Own: Women as Artists* (Thames and Hudson, London, 2000)

P.Z. Brand (ed.), *Beauty Matters* (Indiana University Press, Bloomington and Indianapolis, 2000)

C. Brawer, R. Rosen, et al., *Making Their Mark: Women Artists Move into the Mainstream, 1979–85* (exh. cat., Abbeville Press, New York, 1989)

R. Brilliant, *Portraiture* (Harvard University Press, Cambridge, MA, and London, 1991)

X. Brooke, *Face to Face: Three Centuries of Artists' Self-Portraiture* (exh. cat., Walker Art Gallery, Liverpool, 1994–5)

E. Butler, *From Sketch-Book and Diary* (Adam and Charles Black, London, 1909)

W. Chadwick and I. de Courtivron, *Significant Others: Creativity and Intimate Partnership* (Thames and Hudson, London and New York, 1993)

W. Chadwick (ed.), *Women Artists and the Surrealist Movement* (Thames and Hudson, London, 1985)

—, *Mirror Images: Women, Surrealism and Self-Representation* (MIT Press, Cambridge, MA, and London, 1998)

W. Chadwick, *Women, Art, and Society* (Thames and Hudson, London and New York, revised edition 1997)

—, *Amazons in the Drawing Room: The Art of Romaine Brooks* (exh. cat., National Museum of Women in the Arts, Washington, in conjunction with the University of California Press and Chameleon Books, 2000)

L. De G. Cheney, A.C. Faxon and K. Russo, *Self-Portraits by Women Painters* (Ashgate Publishing, Hants., 2000)

D. Cherry, *Painting Women: Victorian women artists* (Routledge, London, 1993)

J.T. Cohen (ed.), *Insights, Self-Portraits by Women* (David Godine Publisher, Boston, MA, 1978, and Gordon Fraser, London, 1979)

D.P. Corbett and L. Perry (eds.) *English art 1860–1914: Modern artists and identity* (Manchester University Press, Manchester, 2000)

P. Curtis and A.G. Wilkinson, *Barbara Hepworth: A Retrospective* (exh. cat., Tate Liverpool and Art Gallery of Ontario, 1994–5)

M. Cutten and B. Stewart, *The Dictionary of Portrait Painters in Britain up to 1920* (Antique Collectors' Club, Woodbridge, 1997)

B. Dolman, *A Dictionary of Contemporary British Artists* (Antique Collectors' Club, Woodbridge, 1981)

A. Flowers, R. Gibson and E. Lucie-Smith, *Glenys Barton* (Momentum, London, 1997)

A. Fraser, *The Weaker Vessel: Woman's Lot in Seventeenth-Century England* (Weidenfeld & Nicolson, London, 1984)

D. Gaze (ed.), *Dictionary of Women Artists*, Volumes I and II (Fitzroy Dearborn Publishers, London and Chicago, 1997)

P. Gerrish Nunn, *Victorian Women Artists* (The Women's Press, London, 1987)

E. Gombrich, *Art and Illusion* (Oxford University Press, Oxford, 1977)

G. Greer, *The Obstacle Race: The fortunes of women painters and their work* (Secker & Warberg, London, 1979)

M. Holroyd, *Augustus John: The New Biography* (Chatto & Windus, London, 1996)

D.F. Jenkins and C. Langdale, *Gwen John: An Interior Life* (exh. cat., Barbican Art Gallery, 1985)

S. Kelly and E. Lucie-Smith, *The Self-Portrait: A Modern View* (Sarema Press, London, 1987)

L. Knight, *Oil Paint and Grease Paint* (Nicholson & Watson, London, 1936)

M. Meskimmon, *The Art of Reflection: Women Artists' Self-portraiture in the Twentieth Century* (Scarlet Press, London, 1996)

R. Morphet, *EQ Nicholson: designer and painter* (Cygnet Press, London, 1990)

L. Nochlin, *Women, Art, and Power and Other Essays* (Thames and Hudson, New York, 1988)

R. Parker and G. Pollock, *Old Mistresses: Women, Art and Ideology* (Routledge & Kegan Paul, London and Henley, 1981)

A. Penrose, *The Lives of Lee Miller* (Thames and Hudson, London, 1988)

G. Perry (ed.), *Gender and Art* (Yale University Press, New Haven, with the Open University, 1999)

D. Piper, *The English Face* (first published Thames and Hudson, London, 1957; republished National Portrait Gallery, London, 1978, revised 1992)

M. Pointon, *Strategies for Showing: Women, Possession, and Representation in English Visual Culture 1665–1800* (Oxford University Press, Oxford, 1997)

G. Pollock (ed.), *Generations and Geographies in the Visual Arts: Feminist Readings* (Routledge, London and New York, 1996)

C. Reeve, *Mrs Mary Beale, Paintress 1633–1699* (Manor House Museum, Bury St Edmunds, 1994)

W.W. Roworth, *Angelica Kauffmann: A Continental Artist in Georgian England* (exh. cat., the Royal Pavilion, Art Gallery & Museums, Brighton, 1992)

A. Solomon-Godeau, *Photography at the Dock: Essays on Photographic History, Institutions, Practices* (University of Minnesota Press, Minneapolis, 1991)

D. Souhami, *Gluck, 1895-1978: Her Biography* (revised edition, Weidenfeld & Nicolson, London, 2000)

L. Tickner, *The Spectacle of Women: Imagery of the Suffrage Campaign 1907–1914* (University of Chicago Press, Chicago, 1988)

P. Usherwood and J. Spencer-Smith, *Lady Butler Battle Artist 1846–1933* (National Army Museum, London, 1987)

Marie-Louise von Motesiczky: Paintings, Vienna 1925 – London 1985 (exh. cat., Goethe Institut, London, 1985)

G.M. Waters, *Dictionary of British Artists Working 1900–1950* (Eastbourne Fine Art, Eastbourne, 1975)

V. Williams, *Women Photographers: The Other Observers 1900 to the Present* (Virago Press, London, 1986)

The Women's Art Show 1550–1970 (exh. cat., Nottingham Castle Museum, 1982)

C.M. De Zegher, *Inside the Visible: An Elliptical Traverse of Twentieth-Century Art; In, Of and From the Feminine* (MIT Press, Cambridge, MA, and London, 1996)

Websites

Contemporary women artists' practices: web.ukonline.co.uk/n.paradoxa/index.htm

A Directory of Women & the Arts: www.newmexicoranch.com/women/arts

The Fine Art Search Engine: www.artcyclopedia.com/artists/women.html

Grove Dictionary of Art: www.groveart.com

Humanities research with art and art history pages and links: vos.ucsb.edu/shuttle/art.html

Imperial War Museum, London: www.iwm.org.uk

Metropolitan Museum, New York: www.metmuseum.org

Museum of Modern Art, New York: www.moma.org

National Gallery, London: www.nationalgallery.org.uk

National Gallery of Art, Washington, DC: www.nga.gov

National Museum of Women in the Arts: www.nmwa.org

National Portrait Gallery, London: www.npg.org.uk

Tate, London: www.tate.org.uk

Varo Registry – Bibliography of Women Artists: www.varoregistry.com

Women Artists in History: www.wendy.com/women/artists.html

Women's Studies Web Guides: library.gmu.edu/resources/socsci/womenmain.html

Index

Picture credits